Intertextuality and the media

From genre to everyday life

EDITED BY ULRIKE H. MEINHOF
AND JONATHAN SMITH

MANCHESTER UNIVERSITY PRESS
Manchester and New York

distributed exclusively in the USA by St. Martin's Press

Published by Manchester University Press
Oxford Road, Manchester M13 9NR, UK
and Room 400, 175 Fifth Avenue, New York, NY 10010, USA
http://www.manchesteruniversitypress.co.uk

Distributed exclusively in the USA by
St. Martin's Press, Inc., 175 Fifth Avenue, New York, NY 10010, USA

Distributed exclusively in Canada by
UBC Press, University of British Columbia, 2029 West Mall, Vancouver, BC, Canada V6T 1Z2

British Library Cataloguing-in-Publication Data
A catalogue record for this book is available from the British Library

Library of Congress Cataloging-in-Publication Data applied for

ISBN 0 7190 4712 9 *hardback*
     0 7190 4713 7 *paperback*

First published 2000

07 06 05 04 03 02 01 00   10 9 8 7 6 5 4 3 2 1

Typeset in Palatino with Frutiger
by Action Publishing Technology Limited, Gloucester
Printed in Great Britain
by Bell & Bain Limited, Glasgow

INTERTEXTUALITY AND THE MEDIA

MANCHESTER
UNIVERSITY PRESS

Contents

List of illustrations

Photographs from *Spitting Image* are reproduced by kind permission of Central TV

Notes on contributors

Ben Bachmair is Professor of Pedagogy and Media Education at the University Gesamthochschule Kassel. He has published widely on media and education, including (in German) *Fernsehkultur. Subjektivität in einer Welt bewegter Bilder* (Television culture. Subjectivity in a world of moving images) (Opladen: Westdeutscher Verlag, 1996) and (in English) *Interpretative Studies on Children's and Young People's Media Actions* (with Michael Charlton eds) (Munich and New York: Saur Verlag, 1990).

Helen Kelly-Holmes is a lecturer in German and European Studies in the School of Languages and European Studies, Aston University, Birmingham. Her main research, publications and teaching interests include intercultural aspects of market and media discourses and how these relate to identities and perceptions of identities. She is a member of the editorial board of *Current Issues in Language and Society*, for which in 1999 she edited a volume on media discourse (Vol. 5.4: *Multilingual Matters*).

Gunther Kress is Professor of English in Education at the Institute of Education, University of London. He has published in the areas of linguistics, discourse analysis, media and cultural studies, literacy and (visual) semiotics. Books include *Social Semiotics* (Oxford: Polity Press, 1988, with Bob Hodge), *Reading Images: The Grammar of Visual Design* (London: Routledge, 1996, with Theo van Leeuwen), *Learning to Write* (1982), *Before Writing: Rethinking the Paths to Literacy* (1997), *Early Spelling: Between Convention and Creativity* (2000) (all London: Routledge). Among his present interests are connections between education, multimodal representation, learning and aesthetics.

Theo van Leeuwen is Professor of Language and Communication at Cardiff University. He has published widely in the areas of semiotics and discourse analysis. Among his most recent publications are *Reading Images: The Grammar of Visual Design*, co-authored with Gunther Kress (London: Routledge, 1996) and *Speech, Music, Sound* (Basingstoke: Macmillan, 1999).

Ulrike H. Meinhof is Professor of Cultural Studies at the University of Bradford and from January 2001 Professor of German and Cultural Studies at the

University of Southampton. Her research interests are in applied linguistics, media and cultural studies. Books include *Text Discourse and Context: Representations of Poverty in the UK* (Harlow: Longman, 1994, with K. Richardson eds), *Language and Masculinity* (Oxford: Blackwell, 1997, with S. Johnson eds), *Language Learning in the Age of Satellite Television* (Oxford: Oxford University Press, 1999), *Worlds in Common? Television in a Changing Europe* (London: Routledge, 1999, with K. Richardson).

Lothar Mikos is Professor of Media Studies at the Academy for Film and Television at Potsdam-Babelsberg. He is author of several books on film, television and football. Recent publications include *Mattscheibe oder Bildschirm. Asthetik des Fernsehens* (on the aesthetics of television) (co-edited with Joachim von Gottberg and Dieter Weidemann; Berlin: Vistas, 1999) and *Bausteine zu einer Rezeptionsasthetik des Fernsehens* (Towards a reception aesthetic of television) (Berlin: Vistas, 2000). He is working on film and television theory, media education, audience research, popular culture and cultural studies, and qualitative methods in research of media and culture.

Kay Richardson is Senior Lecturer in the School of Politics and Communication Studies at the University of Liverpool. Her main interests are in the study of media discourse, the politics of language and television audience research. Publications include *Nuclear Reactions* (London: John Libbey, 1990, with J. Corner and N. Fenton), *Text Discourse and Context: Representations of Poverty in the UK* (Harlow: Longman, 1994, with U. Meinhof eds), *Worlds in Common? Television in a Changing Europe* (London: Routledge, 1999, with U. Meinhof).

Jonathan Smith is Lecturer in Italian Studies at the University of Wales, Swansea. He has published chiefly on theory and criticism of nineteenth- and twentieth-century Italian and English fiction. His current research concerns the status and functions of narrative and theoretical discourses in contemporary culture, and includes a book project under the title *(Mis)(re)-Cognitions of Other and Self*.

Hans J. Wulff is Professor of Media Studies at the University of Kiel, Germany. His research interest and publications are in the psychology of film and television and in communicative structures of popular culture. Publications include *Psychiatrie im Film* (Psychiatry in film) (Münster: MAKS Publikationen, 1985), *Suspense* ((Mahwah, NJ: Lawrence Erlbaum, 1993), *Darstellen und Mitteilen: Pragmasemiotik des Films* (Performance and communication: pragmasemiotics of the cinema) (Tublingen: Gunter Narr, 1999).

The media and their audience: intertextuality as paradigm

ULRIKE H. MEINHOF AND JONATHAN SMITH

In the various chapters of this book, writers from diverse backgrounds approach media discourse from a variety of angles. However, the individual chapters are brought into cohesive focus by reference to the fuzzy yet powerful term 'intertextuality'. What does this mean?

One principal theme in media studies has long been the analysis of examples of the various genres of media discourse: different kinds of articles in newspapers and other print media, radio and TV programmes (including news, documentaries, drama, game shows and music television), films and videos, advertisements in various media, computer games and so on. However, assembling different studies under the heading of media analysis does not, in itself, create a cohesive theoretical or methodological framework. Indeed, collections of articles on media texts – often using linguistic, semiotic, literary, sociological and other forms of interpretation and analysis side by side with one another – tend to diverge no less substantially in their methodologies than in the types of material considered. The effect of this is often to leave the reader with a potpourri of disconnected accounts of media texts that happen to interest their various authors, who may also in some cases go on to analyse or speculate about a broader audience's responses to such texts. This book is not such a collection.

Each of the chapters in this book is distinctive in its choice of a text or genre as subject matter. These include various different types of printed texts (Kress, Chapter 8), but also a wide range of television programmes such as a game show (Mikos and Wulff, Chapter 6), a satirical series (Meinhof and Smith, Chapter 3), music television (Meinhof and van Leeuwen, Chapter 4), current affairs (Richardson, pter 5) and advertisements (Kelly-Holmes, Chapter 2). The chapters also differ in the ways they define and delimit the object of their analysis, ranging from detailed semiotic readings of text and image on the page (Kress, Chapter 8), to the readings which real-life viewers have provided while engaging with texts (Richardson, Chapter 5, Bachmair, Chapter 7). Why, then, do we claim that such a broad range of different types of discussion is nevertheless not just a haphazard, if interesting, collection of random pieces of analysis? How are they related to each other? And what precisely, then, constitutes an intertextual reading of media discourse? How does such a reading differ from other approaches to interpretation that are less explicitly theorized?

Despite the methodological differences necessarily entailed by their engaging with such a broad range of generic, linguistic, visual and musical encodings, each of our different analyses will be situated within a common theoretical framework to which they all refer. What therefore runs as a connecting thread through all the chapters in the book is the point that each occupies a distinctive position as a particular form of intertextual analysis within a broader field which, between them, they map out. This important point will be developed in the course of the detailed expositions of each chapter, where the individual authors place their textual analyses within the common framework. However, it is also the substantive topic of this introductory chapter. We here attempt to spell out what we mean by intertextuality. This will involve brief consideration of some aspects of the history of the term's development, and a sketch of the range, power and interrelationships of some of the interpretative practices arising from it, including a discussion of some of the difficulties it is sometimes thought to raise. Taken together, the various readings of specific media texts collected in this book aim to contribute to our understanding of media discourse in a range of different forms. However, the collection also offers a theoretical perspective within which these readings can be seen in relation to each other, and aims to provide a context for further work and discussion.

Intertextuality

The term intertextuality was first brought to the notice of a relatively wide readership by Julia Kristeva, who uses it in a number of her writings dating originally from the 1960s and early 1970s (see, for example, Kristeva 1984, and 1986: 35–61). These played an important part in inspiring an extensive body of work in a variety of disciplines, but they did not establish any rigorous or clear sense of the term's definition or application. It is perhaps easiest to grasp something of its force if it is initially approached via a selective account of some of Kristeva's most important intellectual antecedents, and, in particular, the work of the so-called Bakhtin Circle of early twentieth-century Russian semioticians (for a complementary discussion, see also Fairclough 1992: chapter 6).

Within the ambit of Bakhtin Circle semiotics, the issues most relevant here are brought into sharpest focus in a book whose authorship is a matter of dispute, but which was published under Valentin Volosinov's name as *Marxism and the Philosophy of Language* (Volosinov 1973). For instance, Bakhtin/Volosinov proposes that experience itself' exists even for the person undergoing it only in the material of signs', since it could otherwise not be meaningful at all (28–9). On this account, 'consciousness itself can arise … only in the material embodiment [...] of signs'; furthermore, these signs are by definition 'created by an organized group in the process of its social intercourse' (11–13). The following sentences from John Frow's essay 'Intertextuality and ontology' show the closeness of the conceptual (and historical) relationship between the idea of intertextuality and these formulations from Bakhtin/Volosinov:

> In its early elaboration by Kristeva, Barthes and others [the concept of intertextuality] was not restricted to particular textual manifestations of signifying systems but was used, rather, to designate the way in which a culture is structured as a complex network of codes with heterogeneous and dispersed forms of textual realisation. It formulated the codedness or textuality of what had previously been thought in non-semiotic terms (consciousness, experience, wisdom, story, gender, culture, and so on). (Frow 1990: 47)

This replaces the superficial and somewhat obvious observation that all texts contain traces of other texts with a much more complex conception of the interactions between texts, producers of texts and their readers' lifeworlds. Part of the attraction of this kind of conceptual framework is that it enables us to think of media discourse as being qualitatively continuous with the experience of everyday life. In more or less radical ways, all the chapters in this volume explore the consequences of this for analysis of media discourse.

For instance, we shall see that the Meinhof–Smith discussion of the TV series *Spitting Image* (Chapter 3) works with a more restricted definition of intertextuality than do some other chapters. However, even here the analysis turns on the different types of knowledge cross-referenced by different types of viewers in responding to the programme, be it direct personal experience of the parliamentary and electoral processes, learned knowledge of a classic canon of political satire, or a much more widespread, informal (and in this sense popular) knowledge of other TV programmes and their generic formats. It is the possibility of calling on these different types of prior knowledge that makes possible different styles of response channelled by contrasting assumptions that the programme belongs to different genres (be it for example that of political satire, or, as Chapter 3 argues, that of TV pastiche).

Other chapters show how viewers of economic news programmes interpret their viewing by activating various types of knowledge drawn from a variety of other kinds of source (Richardson, Chapter 5), and how the differing responses of viewers to the programme *Rock 'n' Roll Years* draw on their various attitudes, values and memories (Meinhof and van Leeuwen, Chapter 4). Similarly, Mikos and Wulff (Chapter 6) show some of the continuities between social practices in everyday life and the situations re-enacted in game shows, and the subjects of Bachmair's empirical research (Chapter 7) freely associate episodes and themes of their own 'direct' experience with images drawn from the media (photographs, films, TV programmes), thus articulating responses to the latter which appear highly idiosyncratic. Kelly-Holmes's work (Chapter 2) points towards the way in which an entire society's politics (or indeed the politics of more than one society) may become implicated in such a process.

Finally, Kress (Chapter 8) aims to conceptualize a continuous process of semiosis (or production of meanings) in such a way as to minimize the stability of identifiable texts, and therefore also suggest the ultimate redundancy of the term 'intertextuality'. This might, however, be thought to be another way of making a point very similar to the one that we originally (following Frow) presented the term as serving to secure. We therefore need now to look more closely at some of the points of theoretical and methodological contention or confusion that it carries with it.

Some theoretical and methodological issues

Even apart from Kress, it is doubtful whether all contributors to the present volume would assent without reserve to the account of intertextuality we have begun to formulate by reference to work from Bakhtin/Volosinov, Kristeva and Frow. Two sets of issues in particular merit discussion, the first theoretical and the second methodological in nature. From a theoretical point of view, we might seem to be according too exclusive a degree of importance to linguistic and symbolic systems. In the essay we have already cited, Frow has a sentence which brings this point into sharp focus:

> Insofar as the 'real' signified by [...] texts is a moment of signifying process, and indeed is only ever available to knowledge within and by means of a system of representations, it has the form not of the final referent but of a link in an endless chain of semiosis (a chain which may of course be broken for practical purposes and by means of a particular pragmatic delimitation, but in which in principle the 'last instance' of representation is always deferred). (1990: 47)

What might be thought particularly problematic about this is that theory could appear to lose all contact with the data of our own experience if we fail or refuse to recognize that symbolic systems appear quite clearly to be limited in at least two directions. In the first place, the object world to which symbolic systems point or refer is not at all obviously linguistic by nature. Secondly, the deployment of symbolic systems frequently appears to be limited, constrained and on occasion even determined by others – for example, techno-logical, political and economic ones. On the other hand, the purpose of theoretical study is not to ratify the experiences we have already had, but rather to help us understand or explain them in new ways.

Frow himself pursues these arguments through an extensive body of material produced in the course of debates conducted from the mid-1960s to the mid-1980s in the fields of philosophy (Althusser, Derrida) and sociological theory (Laclau and Mouffe), but his discussion is both avowedly and necessarily inconclusive. On the one hand, all such debates are themselves, by definition, located within the symbolic realm, yet on the other, they rapidly reach the point of recognizing that they are also themselves subject to the influences and constraints of extra-symbolic systems. Recognition of facts such as this one, however, is itself precisely an interpretative and therefore symbolic activity. Here again it may be helpful to refer briefly to Bakhtin/Volosinov's *Marxism and the Philosophy of Language* with a view to developing this point and its significance.

Despite its title and some of its rhetoric, much of the content of Bakhtin/Volosinov's book is not obviously compatible with Marxism, and especially not with the orthodox Marxism of its time and place: the Soviet Union, where it was originally published in 1929, having been conceived and written in the years immediately following the Russian Revolution of 1917. The chief point of tension with the Marxist tradition lies in the way the book tends to privilege discursive processes over technological and economic ones in its account of the ways meanings are produced and exchanged. In particular, the points we have already illustrated above with some brief quotations from the book have the further effect that meanings are not understood as being determined once and for all, but as being continually renegotiated in an ongoing dialogical process. These aspects of the book's argument – which are the ones that have made it famous throughout the world – are closer to certain aspects of Nietzsche's thought than they are to Marx's, at least as these two writers have each been widely understood.

For instance, only a few years before, Nietzsche had written that there are no facts, but only interpretations (Nietzsche 1968: 267, section 481). The claim is a famously provocative one, and in itself it is little more than one summative highlight of a programme whose general sense invites us to question both the consistency of the object world of common experience and the patterns of causality presumed to inform it. It is a programme that has engendered disputes continuing up to the present, both as to its meaning and as to the sense in which it could be said to point in the direction of anything that could be considered true (for one relatively recent and sympathetic account, see Vattimo 1988, especially 19–30 and 164–81). Like Bakhtin Circle semiotics, these debates form part of the formative context of the theory of intertextuality, and some of Kristeva's work documents this particularly clearly (see, for example, Kristeva 1986: 35–61, especially 48–52). Although the Bakhtin/Volosinov position is nearer to common-sense interpretations of everyday experience than either is to the more radical interpretations of Nietzsche's philosophy, a number of points that are relevant to our discussion do ensue from this complex constellation of influences.

A first such point is that despite Frow's hedging, the problem of defining the boundaries between language (or more accurately, the realm of discursive or symbolic practices) and material reality was a matter of contention throughout the twentieth century, and remains so. This is the case to such an extent that from some points of view it is not so much the position of the boundary that is in question, as whether it marks a useful distinction at all. We cannot, however, expect to make much progress in understanding the sense or implications of such arguments unless we are prepared to envisage a radical redefinition of terms such as language, discourse or discursive practice. Before moving on to consider some of the more purely methodological issues arising from the use of the term intertextuality, we shall therefore now briefly outline some of the reasons why so crucial a theoretical problem as that of the demarcation of the limits of the linguistic, symbolic or discursive realm cannot be quickly and comfortably settled.

One contribution to this volume – that by Gunther Kress (Chapter 8) – is a small part of a much larger project that has been going on over a period of years, and has attempted to engage in just such a process of radical redefinition as we have suggested be envisaged (see also, for example, Hodge and Kress 1988, Kress and van Leeuwen 1996, Kress 1997). This work has not been done under the institutional banner of philosophy, and its authors are not to be taken for followers of Nietzsche (although it is also worth registering that to whatever extent some of Nietzsche's works have been canonized as classic points of reference for certain kinds of institutionalized philosophy, they were produced by him in tension and conflict with the established academic institutions and discourses of his time; for an accessible historical introduction which also explores the current implications of this point, see Macintyre 1990). However, it is worth noting that the book by Hodge and Kress just cited – designed to provide specialists in a broad range of fields with a 'usable, critical theory of language' (Hodge and Kress 1988: vii) – includes an important annotated bibliography of material relevant to the development of its argument (268–72). This lists – among others – a number of works by authors (Deleuze and Guattari, Derrida, Foucault and Lyotard as well as Kristeva herself) who have come much closer to a radical interpretation of Nietzsche than do Bakhtin/Volosinov. We cannot review this complex and extensive literature here, but we do wish to underline – heavily – the degree to which current conceptions of language (including its limits) are open to criticism and revision, the amount of work that remains to be done in this area, and also the extent to which relevant work already done awaits effective dissemination. This last points means in turn that much more is at stake in the way we choose to define language (or whatever terms we might then choose to substitute for that one) than a simple point of definition. To illustrate this, let us return to Bakhtin/Volosinov.

We do not mean to suggest by any of our remarks up to this point that *Marxism and the Philosophy of Language* is any more purely faithful to Nietzsche than it is to Marx. Far from it (and one implication of the theory of intertextuality is indeed that we delude ourselves if we imagine that we know what pure fidelity to any kind of textual authority would be). Nor shall we attempt to explore in any degree of detail the ramifications of the history of the reading of Marx or Nietzsche. However, as we have already said, *Marxism and the Philosophy of Language* consistently privileges discursive processes over economic and technological ones in its accounts of the production of meaning, and this order of priorities does place the book closer to Nietzsche than to Marx as these two thinkers have very commonly been understood, and as they were widely understood in Bakhtin/Volosinov's and also Kristeva's intellectual environments. Kristeva's own cross-referencing of Nietzsche and Bakhtin noted above is the work of an exile from the Soviet bloc; markedly so, since Nietzsche's thought was in fact widely considered to be the very antithesis of Marxism until long after the publication of the Bakhtin/Volosinov book in the Soviet Union. Attempts to yoke elements of each to the other came later, and, being highly unorthodox from a Marxist point of view, were generally undertaken in the West (Vattimo 1993, first published in Italy in 1979, shows traces of a project of this kind which in fact dates back to the very early 1970s). To whatever extent Bakhtin/Volosinov's title and some of the earlier sections of the book's argument appear to conflict with its sense as we have outlined it above, it is at least likely that this arrangement was adopted partly as a deliberate attempt to evade the unfavourable attention of the Soviet authorities, and that any least hint of a debt to Nietzsche's thought or of an affinity with it was avoided for similar reasons.

It is also the case, however, that this book, like much of the work of the Bakhtin Circle, is marked by the academic neo-Kantian philosophy of its time, and that this too plays a part in blunting the force of its redefinition of language and of any claim for its central importance. In other words, we can generalize and say that the ways in which we think about language and discuss it may be subject to powerful social, political and institutional constraints, but these will not always be brought to bear in obviously dramatic ways: Bakhtin and Volosinov worked within an intellectual tradition that probably played a part no less significant than that of the Soviet regime in limiting the force and range of the theory they developed. In this specific instance, a message that was to prove influential did slip through the net, although it was never very widely broadcast in the Soviet Union in the authors' lifetimes, and was in any case somewhat muted relative to subsequent ones along comparable lines that it played some part in inspiring. However, in other circumstances than the very particular ones in which Bakhtin and Volosinov worked, this issue presents itself in somewhat different ways.

Our current ideas about language are supported by the prestige and inertia of our educational practices and institutions, and by the heavy investments made in them by societies and political systems that would be forced to countenance major and decisive changes if that prestige and inertia were to be seriously eroded. Conversely, a large part of the point of Kress's attempts to reconceptualize 'language' is to provide the bases for a rethinking of what effective education might entail in the twenty-first century (see Kress 1997 in particular). Thus, if his approach and style of discussion (and possibly those of some other contributors to this volume) are unfamiliar and challenging, that is partly because of the deeply entrenched modes of thought that we bring to the encounter with them, and because those happen to be the modes of thought we have inherited. This is a very different thing from saying that such modes of thought are necessarily the best ones available or possible, and the point should be considered before it is casually concluded that the theory of intertextuality or its offshoots have been too ambitious or extreme in the range of phenomena and questions (including those of the nature and limits of language, or the boundary between the discursive and extra-discursive realms) that they have sought to show in a new light. It is, however, also partly for reasons of this kind that such theories can generally only advance piecemeal and case by case.

One important reason for combining a theoretical interest in the (re-)definition of language and intertextuality with a case-study approach to media texts is that this will ground the discussion in a more practical and applied context than would otherwise be available. Fairclough (1992 and 1995) provides ample exemplification of intertextual readings of media texts, although these are limited to the work of the analyst, and do not extend to considering the range of meanings produced by other readers and viewers of the texts discussed. By contrast, the various contributions to this volume were selected precisely because they illustrate and pursue aspects of the theoretical question how to define, expand or delimit an object of analysis from a number of different directions, including the standpoint of actual readers and viewers in varying social circumstances (see especially Chapters 4, 5 and 7).

A second type of major difficulty widely thought to be raised by the notion of intertextuality is of a more narrowly methodological nature. It has indeed been pointed out in criticism of Kristeva's own work in this area that she herself drew attention to its ambiguity, yet without doing anything to resolve the practical difficulties this causes (see, for example, Culler 1981: 106–7). Even in Kristeva's own usage, as well as subsequently, the term's scope has often been reductively limited to pinpoint specific identifiable texts whose relation with each other is alleged to determine their meaning, rather than designating the much more diffuse cultural space (which has been the principal focus of our discussion up to this point) within and by reference to which textual meanings are constructed. In a book that sometimes echoes and sometimes diverges from his essay 'Intertextuality and ontology' on which we drew above, Frow makes these very different emphases explicit by using the contrasting terms 'precise' and 'diffuse' intertextuality (Frow 1986: 155). This distinction is, however, a much weaker one than it first appears. Despite being all but exclusively literary in its frame of reference, Culler's discussion of intertextuality recognizes that the former is in practice an instance of the latter: 'what makes possible reading and writing is not a single anterior action which serves as origin [...] but an open series of acts which work together to constitute something like a language: discursive possibilities, systems of convention, clichés and descriptive systems' (Culler 1981: 110).

Media texts (which for this reason furnish the general theory of intertextuality with some fundamentally important points of reference) illustrate particularly well the disparate and heterogenous processes described by Culler, because they are in many cases essentially multimodal. This is to say that many media texts exist in, and make use of, what we shall call several different semiotic modes at the same time. Among these different semiotic modes, spoken and written text, visual images and music are the most clearly defined. This multimodality is clearly a very different thing from remodelling a source text A in a subsequent text B. This is one reason why it is important here to understand, as Frow puts it in 'Intertextuality and ontology', that

> intertextual analysis is distinguished from source criticism both by this stress on interpretation rather than on the establishment of particular facts, and by its rejection of a unilinear causality (the concept of 'influence') in favour of an account of the work performed upon intertextual material and its functional integration in the later text. (Frow 1990: 46)

We may take this as a cue to use the term intertextuality to refer to the process of viewers and readers interpreting texts which exhibit the dynamic interactivity of several semiotic modes, and interpreting them in ways that are partially controlled by this multimodality.

A clear illustrative example of this is provided by the way we react to images on the screen. A single scene may be interpreted by viewers as being tense, melancholy, cheerful, terrifying or just banal if it is shown with a series of different musical accompaniments. Similarly, as Meinhof and van Leeuwen report in Chapter 4, viewers of *Rock 'n' Roll Years* who had reacted negatively to violent images of the events of May 1968 in Paris when watching them without sound, saw the same sequence in a favourable light – as being vivacious and energetic – when they saw it a second time, accompanied by the Rolling Stones soundtrack 'Jumping Jack Flash'. Another example, closer to the themes of Gunther Kress's discussion in Chapter 8, might be the effects of an article in the press in determining the way readers will interpret an accompanying photograph, and vice versa.

Another dimension of intertextuality is the relationship between text and audience. This is less specific to the media of mass communication, but it is no less important than multimodality and indeed interacts with it. In this connection, what has sometimes appeared to be a problem – but is in practice the source of the term's power – is the question which arises as to the aptness, legitimacy or authority of the analyst's attempt to identify the relevant precise intertextual reference. Out in the world, people other than analysts are applying a variety of other standards of relevance all the time, and it is for reasons of this kind that analysis in terms of precise intertextual relations is sometimes thought to be arbitrary or restrictive. This is precisely what meshes the theoretical issues raised in the previous section with the methodological ones posed here: so far from making the notion of intertextuality inoperable, as is sometimes thought, they mark out the areas where it brings into relation with each other a variety of styles of analysis, some bearing more upon audience response, its mechanisms or its conditions than upon the text itself, conceived as a static entity.

What Frow calls diffuse intertextuality can be thought of in a variety of different ways, ranging from absolute idiosyncrasy in the construction of precise intertextual relations at one extreme, to the most inelastically classificatory notion of genre – something the notion of intertextuality is designed to avoid – at the other. Bachmair's contribution to this volume (Chapter 7) thematizes highly idiosyncratic modes of reception of the first-mentioned kind: the emphasis is on the way individual viewers studied by Bachmair and his team of researchers integrate media images into their personal lives. This brings to light the production of meanings which are highly unpredictable from the researchers' point of view, but become largely perspicuous when the subject's biography is taken into account.

This means that intertextual analysis cannot locate a given text within the confines of a single specified genre. In general terms, we can say that texts carry multiple traces of various other texts of disparate kinds, and on the basis of such tracings they are ascribed to genres; but on the basis of the multiplicity of such tracings they may be ascribed to various distinct genres. In the specific cases studied by Bachmair, the sheer idiosyncrasy of his subjects' decoding procedures, and of the points of reference they use, virtually annihilate the notion of genre altogether. Thus Bachmair's contribution shows that while on the one hand genre is the principal mediating concept which serves to locate a particular text within the general intertextual field, the notion of genre is on the other hand little more than an analytical fiction whose purpose it is to explain the possibility of less idiosyncratic modes of perception. The chapters preceding Bachmair's are devoted to exploring from different angles some of the ways in which the field of intertextuality or semiosis is segmented and partially controlled by a variety of generic formats and media of mass communication. Bachmair's own chapter in this volume is just one among the products of an extensive programme of educational research which engages closely with the frame of reference of Kress's broader project outlined above (pp. 7–9). It is against this kind of background that this collection as a whole aims, through a multifaceted series of illustrative analyses, to stimulate reflection (and doubt) about the categories and terms available to contemporary studies of language and the media.

Before moving to a chapter-by-chapter outline, we must however – as editors – sound a note of caution. The notion of intertextuality is a powerful analytical tool for all the reasons we have outlined in the hope of drawing attention to its value. Yet even here – to repeat something already said above – we do not have the scope to bring out the full extent of its force and range. These therefore demand further exploration and debate before it is concluded either that they are more limited than we seek to suggest (as might be the case if too restricted a notion of text is assumed) or that some applications of the notion exaggerate the degree of freedom to shape and produce meaning that exists in contemporary societies.

Mikos and Wulff still work in Chapter 6 with a complementary *ad hoc* notion of 'intersituativity' which at the same time stresses the textuality of situations in the TV studio and in viewers' more direct experience that are not normally understood as being texts, and also conserves a residual sense of these situations being experienced as material, non-textual, situations. For so long as the full implications for our social and personal existence of such broader projects as those of Bachmair and Kress are not widely understood, it may be that this kind of precarious terminological balance does as much justice as can be done to the awkward lack of fit between theoretical and everyday experience, just because of the way it seems to limit the former. One reason for making this point is that a contrary emphasis, such as Bachmair's, on the idiosyncrasy of the meanings produced by media audiences might occasionally appear (if it were ungenerously misconstrued) to suggest that viewers have unlimited freedom in this regard, and therefore that all is well in contemporary media-rich societies. This is far from being the case, and we therefore urge our readers to approach this book as a supplement to other work and other kinds of work on the media, rather than as displacing or replacing such material. For those insufficiently grounded in media studies to be able to maintain this kind of balance independently, we would accordingly suggest that they read it alongside a more general introduction to the subject. One such work, which opens with an important review of current notions of communication – interpersonal, through the media, and elsewhere – is Stuart Price's stimulating book *Media Studies* (1993).

Chapter-by-chapter synopsis

In Chapter 2 Helen Kelly-Holmes focuses on three advertisements for Irish-branded beers, to investigate the interrelation between intertextuality and the formation of national and cultural identities. She argues that contemporary commercial texts draw on many different narratives and myths of Irishness whose contradictions and inconsistencies undermine older hierarchical certainties about what constituted Irishness and Irish culture. The inconsistencies of these 'unofficial' texts offer mutable, depoliticized versions of Irish identity which are more positive and, ironically, less stereotypical than the crude cliché linking Irishness – for the English – with violence and terrorism.

Chapter 3, by Ulrike Meinhof and Jonathan Smith, begins with a reassessment of generic classifications of the popular British TV programme *Spitting Image* as political satire. Partly because it has made frequent use of puppets representing well-known figures from political life – and also because it frequently makes reference to news and current affairs – a generic classification as political satire seems an obvious one. However, the chapter argues that these political figures blend into the spectrum of characters seen on television, because they appear alongside many other puppets which represent real and fictional characters from a wide range of other TV programmes and genres. Rather than being political satire, *Spitting Image* dramatizes instead an interplay of generic TV formats. This indiscriminate straddling and effacement of the boundaries of genres echoes and dramatizes the unpredictability of the processes of reception described by Bachmair. The effect is a kind of generalized TV pastiche, a fictionalized version of the entanglement of media texts with direct lived experience.

Chapter 4, by Ulrike Meinhof and Theo van Leeuwen, focuses

on the series *Rock 'n' Roll Years*. Exploiting heavily the televisual possibilities of multimodality, this programme is even more of a generic hybrid than is *Spitting Image*. By juxtaposing a soundtrack featuring a selection of rock and roll music from a particular year with frequently memorable news clips from the same year, the programme defies clear-cut genre expectations – is it a news compilation with musical accompaniment or an illustrated music programme? The alignment of musical and verbal phrasings of popular songs with news images from the same year has calculated functions of commenting – sometimes ironically – on images and news stories, but also of supplying these with mood and atmosphere. However, these different combinations of different types of coding are not the sole factors in the production of meaning: viewers interviewed base their responses on a variety of different social and cultural resources selected according to their social and political background, age and cultural tastes.

In Chapter 5 Kay Richardson focuses entirely on viewers' responses as they attempt to make sense of a television genre which most viewers experience as being difficult: that of economic news. Richardson discusses the character of the resources which viewers use in attempting to make sense of such news programmes. The emphasis here is on the intertextual complexity of viewer discourse about such news. Richardson distinguishes between three types of resources which viewers draw on: first, extra-textual resources which are explicitly intertextual, such as references to the press, television and books. Secondly, those which have a more abstract character, such as 'general knowledge' – which must be derived from other texts but is not represented as being so by the viewers studied. A third category of resources derives more directly and explicitly from personal experience.

In Chapter 6 Lothar Mikos and Hans-Jürgen Wulff again emphasize the continuities between everyday experiences and situations and those produced for television. Their case study of the TV game show *Wheel of Fortune* shows entertainment TV to be a multi-dimensional cultural practice. The concept of intertextuality is complemented here by the neologism 'intersituativity' to point to a whole network of situations linking the players in the studio with the viewers at home in ways that exceed the limits of language and text as these are conventionally understood.

Chapter 7, by Ben Bachmair, takes the analysis of this interconnection between media and everyday life to its furthest point. Here, viewers' discourse shows only the most highly personal and strongly encoded references to media material (which the analysis therefore struggles in some instances to identify). Differentiating between two sharply contrasting ways in which people make meanings in the context of everyday life, Bachmair shows through case studies that rather than reproducing or repeating textual meanings (mimesis), individuals create their own meanings by incorporating a wide range of symbolic material into their own everyday performances (poiesis). Bachmair concludes by stressing the importance of lifestyle – that is, a horizontal rather than a vertical and hierarchical differentiation – as the new form of social demarcation.

In the final chapter Gunther Kress aims to challenge the category of intertextuality by suggesting that it exists to patch up a problem caused by starting with the wrong theory (of text and language) in the first place. Discussing a set of texts ranging from a pamphlet about the poll tax to a child's simulation of a newspaper, Kress argues that they function as mere punctuations of a continuous process of semiosis – that is, as temporary realizations of meaning in language and other semiotic forms. Kress's ultimate demand is for a wholesale revision of existing categories of text, genre and language with a view to constructing a new, more inclusive and more dynamic theory of semiosis.

References

Culler, J. (1981), *The Pursuit of Signs*, London: Routledge & Kegan Paul.
Fairclough, N. (1992), *Discourse and Social Change*, Oxford: Polity Press.
—— (1995), *Media Discourse*, London: Arnold.
Frow, J. (1986), *Marxism and Literary History*, Oxford: Blackwell.
—— (1990), 'Intertextuality and ontology', in M. Worton and J. Still (eds), *Intertextuality: Theories and Practices*, Manchester: Manchester University Press, 45–55.
Hodge, R. and Kress, G. (1988), *Social Semiotics*, Oxford: Polity Press.
Kress, G. (1997), *Before Writing*, London: Routledge.
—— and van Leeuwen, T. (1996), *Reading Images*, London: Routledge.
Kristeva, J. (1984), *Revolution in Poetic Language*, New York: Columbia University Press.
—— (1986), *The Kristeva Reader*, Oxford: Blackwell.
Macintyre, A. (1990), *Three Rival Versions of Moral Enquiry*, London: Duckworth.
Nietzsche, F. (1968), *The Will to Power*, New York: Vintage Books.
Price, S. (1993), *Media Studies*, Harlow: Longman.

Vattimo, G. (1988), *The End of Modernity*, Oxford: Polity Press.
—— (1993), *The Adventure of Difference*, Oxford: Polity Press.
Volosinov, V. (1973), *Marxism and the Philosophy of Language*, Cambridge, MA: Harvard University Press.

2

'Strong words softly spoken': advertising and the intertextual construction of 'Irishness'

HELEN KELLY-HOLMES

In this chapter the intertextual construction of Irishness is explored, with particular reference to the role of advertising in this process. First of all, the notion of an intertextual hierarchy which, until recently, could be said to have prescribed Irishness is examined; then the current situation, whereby this notional hierarchy has been replaced by a horizontal intertextuality, is analysed. The role of commercial texts in the intertextual construction of Irishness is next highlighted before three advertising texts are examined in an attempt to illustrate how such texts are both product and producer of this intertextuality.

Texts, 'Irishness' and Irish identities

The fundamental features of national identity as outlined by Smith (1991) include a historic territory or homeland, common myths and historical memories, a common, mass public culture, common legal rights and duties and a common economy (p. 14). Linking all of these aspects – both with each other and with the individuals who assume the national identity in question – is a range of texts and intertextual relationships. Identity – national, regional and local – depends on texts as a source of legitimacy. Even where the individual has never actually read texts such as the French Declaration of Human Rights, the German Basic Law or *Grundgesetz*, or the famous Fifth Amendment to the American Constitution, they represent a key reference point for the formation and reinforcement of national identity. On the one hand, in an obvious way, they are paraded as symbols of the nation or community; on the other, such texts form the basis of the culture-specific legal, educational and political system, thus contributing in a less overt but no less powerful way to a shared sense of identity. In addition to these authoritative 'founding' texts of the nation or community there are the deliberate identity-forming texts of public broadcasting and political speeches.

The inherent assumptions about identity and the act of sharing a range of public texts circulating in any society perhaps contribute most to a common identity. As Anderson (1981), Hobsbawm (1990) and Billig (1995) have pointed out, the effect of deliberate propaganda is not nearly as significant as the ability of the mass media to involve individuals on a day-to-day basis in the act of sharing a common set of texts, such as the evening news, soap operas, etc., in the process of identity formation in today's society. Furthermore, in any attempt to construct national identities, texts can be employed to define and prescribe such identities – for example, in the Irish case, to show individuals how to be 'Irish', what 'Irishness' is. Such texts and intertextual relations can in turn form the basis for 'fixed' or 'accepted' texts of 'Irishness', written and read externally.

In the years following political independence from the UK, the texts defining 'Irishness' and contributing to the construction of Irish identity can be seen to have been narrowly prescribed and laid down by the cultural, political, administrative, religious and educational elites in Irish society. There existed in the Republic an invisible but pervasive intertextual hierarchy of what we shall term 'foundational', 'official' and 'unofficial' texts. The 'foundational' texts, defined here as those which mark and symbolize the founding of the nation and which are overtly tied to national identity, would – in the Irish context – include the Proclamation of Independence, the Constitution, the National Anthem. They represented the textual bedrock upon which 'official texts', understood here as the texts of the administrative, religious and educational institutions, were based. In turn, the 'unofficial' everyday texts at the bottom of this hierarchy, such as journalistic texts, public and private discussions, undirected media and advertising texts, could be seen to rely on the givens and assumptions of these official texts. Thus, a vertical intertextuality can be seen to have formed the context for the process of identity formation, as well as prescriptions of 'Irishness'.

The notion of this hierarchy, although useful, is of course necessarily simplistic, since it implies an identifiable starting-point and only relates to how 'Irishness' was prescribed, how individuals were expected to construct their identity, namely through a type of ritu-alized and passive reading. In reality, of course, individuals wrote their own texts and lived out contradictory and subversive exis-tences within the prescribed hierarchy. However, such a notion is still valid and useful in explaining how 'Irishness' was defined inter-nally and was described externally.

A good example of this prescribed hierarchical intertextuality is 'the right to life', as guaranteed in the foundational text of the 1936 Constitution. This was given expression and application in the texts of school books, diocesan letters and hospital charters. These 'offi-cial texts' in turn formed the basis for people's everyday experience of such an issue and were assumed to be taken as givens in public and private discussions (for example, a radio programme about abortion), thus prescribing that aspect of 'Irishness' (that is, atti-tudes to abortion).

This hierarchical relationship was symptomatic of an inevitable stage in the development of a new national identity, the time when the need for a coherent spirit to support the national project was felt most. In the simplistic hierarchical intertextuality of the nation state, texts were read as given, without the possibility of writing new ones that described a complex and contradictory reality (cf. O'Toole 1997a).

Until relatively recently, the nature and range of the texts presuming to define 'Irishness' and, in turn, construct Irish identity, could be 'controlled'. Although there was some intentional control in the form of explicit censorship, the variety was largely limited by lack of access to texts originating outside the national or regional sphere. However, such factors as access to British terrestrial televi-sion and other media, the growth in satellite television and other transnational forces have all meant that the unofficial texts have changed radically over the last twenty years and can no longer be limited or defined – intentionally or unintentionally.

Neither can their intertextual relations with official and foun-dational texts. In the same period a move away from this hierarchical intertextual structure, in which the order and nature of the relationship between foundational, official and unofficial texts was strictly defined, has been witnessed. Today a complex, hori-zontal intertextuality has replaced the rigid simplicity of the hierarchical intertextuality and this reflects much more the every-day reality of the lived experience. This concept of horizontal intertextuality – although again necessarily simplistic – is useful in describing the situation whereby individuals, groups and institutions are able to choose and combine aspects of texts from a variety of sources in whatever way they please – that is, without the imposition of a prescribed hierarchy of foundational, official and unofficial texts. Thus, this horizontal intertextual process negates the vertical intertextual hierarchy, and texts can be used and even subverted in a variety of new contexts. This process may in turn result in new notions of 'Irishness' and contribute to the construction of new Irish identities, something that invariably leads to new and contradictory relationships. A good example here is the Proclamation of Independence, one of the 'sacred' foundational texts which not only formed the basis for the modern Irish state but has also fed the myth of the 1916 Rising and the Republican movement and their texts. Today this text, whilst still fulfilling these prescribed roles, is also found on display in every Irish pub, as part of the decor – its political (and violent) associations diluted by its presence in the commercial context of 'Irishness'. Thus, intertextually, its role in this hierarchy has been diluted; it has instead become one among many possible texts in a horizontal relationship. In the context of the Irish pub its emblematic meaning is created through intertextual linkage with the commercial texts of 'Irishness'.

This evolution from vertical to horizontal intertextuality in the construction of 'Irishness' and Irish identities can be seen not only to result *in* contradictions but also to result *from* the contradiction between the prescribed texts of 'Irishness' and the reality of experience, particularly the lived experience of emigration, of living a hybridized and hyphenated existence. The writing of Irish identity in texts has now been reclaimed from the political, educational and cultural elites and this opens up not only the possibility of new texts, but also new sources from which those texts will emerge and be chosen. As James (1996) points out, the 'postmodern' nation 'is increasingly experienced as an unstructured, and at times even optional, background choice' (p. 35) and it is within such a context that horizontal intertextuality functions.

The hybridization of identity through the act of choosing from possibilities rather than simply taking on the straitjacket of an identity through reading the given texts is exemplified by the case of religion in Irish society today. Religious texts – primarily those of the Catholic church, but also by implication the texts of the other churches and concerning the interaction between all these and the state – were seen to be a constant and reassuring source of 'Irishness', prescribing the identity through the reading of such texts. However, the writing of a new text, namely divorce legislation, by the secular side of Irish identity, describes the new relationship with the Church and a fundamental change in the 'Catholic' nature of Irish identity (cf. O'Toole 1997a). What is perhaps of most interest here is not that the divorce text has been written, but that many Catholics who voted for divorce continue to attend mass and to read the texts given by the Catholic Church and that they do not accept that this is a contradiction. This, too, points to the breakdown of hierarchical intertextuality. Irish people today appear to pick and choose from a range of texts in constructing their religious, social, cultural, political (etc.) identity, without adhering – or feeling that they have to adhere – to a prescribed intertextual relationship which defines 'Irishness' in terms based in the foundational text of the constitutional ban on divorce.[1]

Another fixed tenet of 'Irishness' was the Northern Ireland conflict and its texts.[2] The 'Irish' relationship with Northern Ireland, or 'the North' as it is referred to in these texts, was assumed to be that of sympathy with at least the Nationalist if not the Republican cause. The basis for this was, again, the foundational text of the Constitution with its aspiration towards 'a united Ireland' and its declared claim on the geographical area of Northern Ireland. This in turn filtered through, intertextually, to official (for example, educational) and unofficial texts. However, such a reading is no longer a given in the construction of 'Irishness' or the prescription of an Irish identity, owing in large part to the fact that this given began to be questioned by unofficial texts, mainly journalistic and media texts. This example, together with the case of divorce legislation, show how far this vertical relationship has broken down, since, in fact, in both cases it is the unofficial texts which have resulted in changes in the official and ultimately the foundational texts through referenda to alter the Constitution. Thus, the foundational texts, far from prescribing the hierarchical intertextual relationship, have themselves become vulnerable and subject to change in the horizontal intertextual process within which any text can affect or alter any other text.

This horizontal intertextuality involves an acceptance of contradictions and a rejection of certainties which were such a key feature of a prescribed 'Irishness' in the early years of the state. For example, the certainty that 'Irish' implied all things that were not British – which also limited the Irish understanding of 'Britishness', confining it to a limiting stereotype of 'Englishness' (cf. Kiberd 1996, Kearney 1997, O'Toole 1997a). The reality, the lived experience of the Anglo-Irish relationship is, however, evidenced in the hybrid texts that describe it, rather than in the prescribed, read-only texts that ordain it. As Kearney rightly points out, citizens of the UK and Ireland are 'mongrelised, interdependent, impure, mixed up' (1997: 188). The relationship with Britain and its role in Irish identity has often been described as the association between the 'self and anti-self' (cf. Kearney 1997). Beyond even the extremely complex political and post-colonial level, both countries are inextricably linked at the level of family, economy, language, travel, etc., but these links are fractured and painful in the way only relationships between close relatives can be. The articulation and acknowledge-ment of this lived reality changes fundamentally the relationship between the texts which have formed the bedrock of Irish identity. The tension and contradiction inherent in the relationship is illus-trated by the fact that probably the two most frequent collocations of the adjective 'Irish' in texts which the British public encounter are 'Irish terrorist' and 'Irish pub'.

Parallel to these developments has been a mushrooming of crit-ical texts about 'Irishness', which not only seek to explain the changing construction of Irish identities and 'the growing popular-ity of all things Irish' (Guinness 1996) but also set the context for this new identity by questioning notions of 'Irishness' and its prescribed texts. Historian Joe Lee's seminal study of the Republic since its foundation, for instance, dealt with, among other things, the bitter-ness of the Irish experience of emigration, hypothesizing that the tragic attitude of Ireland to its emigrants hypocritically hid the state's (and general population's) actual relief that so many were willing to leave so that the few remaining would not have to share – thus breaking down a number of intertextual links and givens in 'Irishness' and Irish identity. This paved the way for a number of works, academic, fictional and journalistic, which have chronicled the new Ireland and its identities[3] and have led to a hotly contested debate. For instance, the cultured world of critic and journalist Fintan O'Toole, who promotes a civilized, tolerant and open society, is anathema to others such as maverick journalist and writer

John Waters, who sees O'Toole as part of 'official Ireland' – middle-class, urbane people who have lost their roots. In his texts Waters promotes and praises small-town Ireland, 'the bog'. Equally, in such texts, there is disagreement over where Ireland belongs or rather should belong. Luke Gibbons's view that 'Ireland is a first world country, but with a third world memory' (1996: 3) is disputed by those who aspire to membership of the former. Roddy Doyle's[4] fiction forms a huge part of these critical texts, forcing the nation to look at much that it would rather ignore.

Advertising texts and 'Irishness'

In contemporary consumer society, advertising and other market-ing texts constitute a not insignificant component of the texts in circulation which contribute to the portrayal and creation of identi-ties. In Ireland and outside of Ireland, 'Irish' marketing texts – in particular advertising for tourist products, alcohol and other stereo-typically 'Irish' goods – have not only been defined by, but have also come to define 'Irishness' and Irish identities.

The landscape of the west of Ireland, the mythical and mystical coast immortalized in the texts of writers such as Heinrich Böll,[5] provides a good illustration. This has become a given in the texts promoting Irish products, mainly tourist texts, as the following examples show:

> The beauty of Ireland is legendary. From the green pastures to the deep moody lakes and the wild rolling hills. (Irish Tourist Board 1996b)

> *Ireland at its most Irish*
> Old ways and customs still thrive in the west of Ireland … Traditions apart, it is also an area of haunting beauty. (Stena Line 1997)

> Remote and untamed, wild and windswept – no region has provided as much inspiration to the great writers … and holiday-makers … as Ireland's west coasts. (Thomas Cook 1997)

The rugged landscape of the west of Ireland was, however, not always so revered. In previous centuries and in other texts it was maligned for the frugal living it provided and the forced emigration which it indirectly caused. However, in tourist texts we do not hear the 'anonymous quotations' (Barthes 1981a) of these emigrants or of those who died of starvation; instead it is the uniform voice of the admiring visitor. It can be seen, therefore, that intertextual interaction with marketing texts has thus played a key role in the formation of this aspect of 'Irishness' and Irish identity, in a continuous and reflexive process. For many Irish people, their first realization of the beauty and 'value' of the landscape was not through the direct, everyday contact with it, but rather through the intense encounter with the commercial text – the postcard, the collage of images set to music, the advertisement – and the consequent recognition that the culture had 'value'.

The notion of an Irish cuisine, as promoted by, in particular, another notional construct, the Irish pub, provides another illustration. The texts of the Irish pub tell us that 'Few other countries enjoy such a high reputation for quality of home grown produce' (Guinness, no date) and this image has been used to promote food products abroad. This cuisine and its texts have been carefully cultivated by the tourist industry to match the evaluation by tourists and observers of Ireland as a place where food should be pure and natural due to the nature of the landscape and – up to recently – the underdeveloped infrastructure. In turn, these texts have not only fed on but also fed back into a new set of prescribed texts defining 'Irishness', which is presumed in the production of yet more commercial texts, for instance: 'Ireland enjoys the distinction of producing some of the finest food and drink in the world' (Irish Tourist Board 1996b).

Guinness and its texts form both the basis for and the intertextual link between all of these advertising and promotional texts. The product most widely identified as 'Irish' is Guinness. To quote from the company's PR material, '*Guinness* is synonymous with Ireland – an emotional and symbolic icon of its culture, an atmospheric reflection of the country's rare beauty, a joyous celebration of Ireland's finest qualities' (Guinness, no date).

Interestingly, the case of Guinness and its identity illustrate the complexity of the notion of 'Irishness'. The company was set up wo hundred years ago by the Anglo-Irish Protestant Arthur Guinness, and today this international company operates largely from its London headquarters. However, in commercial texts, 'Irishness' is an inherent feature of Guinness and vice versa: 'It's part of what we [Irish] are' (Hill 1997).

Guinness has produced some of the most creative advertising

texts to appear on British and Irish television and the Guinness advertising account is 'the jewel in the crown ... the most prized account in the industry' (Green 1996). The approach is interesting in that the 'Irishness' is rarely explicit in the sophisticated television campaigns, but certain intangible 'Irish' qualities are, though inter-textual links, invoked or alluded to – for example, intellectualism, poetry, friendliness, mysticism, as in, for instance, the esoteric and highly successful 'heart of darkness' campaign featuring quirky actor Rutger Hauer. The series, designed by London-based Ogilvy and Mather, featured scenes from a cornfield, the belly of a whale and a surreal trip inside a pint of stout. In the more recent 'black and white' campaign the team at O & M felt it was 'vital to get the cryptic tone just so' (Green 1996). On the other hand, through its Irish pub concept and through local campaigns, Guinness associates itself directly with Ireland and promotes a rather old-fashioned stereotype of the country which, it could be argued, observes the vertical intertextuality outlined above. For example, very simple and unsophisticated Guinness posters appear in Birmingham in March to wish people (Irish or otherwise) a happy St Patrick's Day. Thus, we see another feature of the hybridized identity based on a renegotiated horizontal intertextuality in the form of old and new notions and texts of 'Irishness' co-existing rather than schizophreni-cally competing.

Although these marketing texts are relatively new, the product of the last twenty years or so, they are fed by many of the founda-tional texts of the nation and also by the texts used and organized for the purposes of national identity, such as the selected texts of the literary revival of the late 1800s and – perhaps more importantly – the texts written about them. The simplicity of the marketing texts and their reading of this 'canon' hide the very great differences between its members and deny the legitimacy of a contradictory writing. A good example is a calendar of Irish writers found in all major tourist outlets. Here 'Irish' writers are all lumped together, harmoniously composing the Irish literary canon – a continuous, harmonious and chronological text. The following quote from the Irish Tourist Board's 1996 literature for the German market illus-trates this crude packaging of the Irish literary canon: 'Irish writers and poets such as Shaw, Joyce & Co.[6] have long been standards of literary history' (Irish Tourist Board 1996a). Note also the obser-vance of a strict, linear and smooth intertextual chronology in the following quote: 'Most notably the Irish way with words resulted in a tradition of play-writing and story-telling, which gave the world literary giants like Swift, Sheridan, Wilde, Joyce and O'Casey' (Irish Tourist Board 1996b).

It is, however, the stereotype of the literary nation and its texts that have done most to improve the image of 'Irishness' and to promote a positive construction of Irish identity globally. Texts about this canon have come to form the foundational texts of not only a marketed culture, but also an identity people can adopt at will. As Irish writer Joseph O'Connor points out, the literary tradition has come to be used by the Irish in Britain as a positive counterpart to the drunken stereotype and as a source of self-confidence (O'Connor 1994: 152).

Intertextuality and 'Irishness' in advertising

The aim of investigating these advertisements is to see what role they play in intertextual constructions of Irishness, how they relate (intertextually) to the prescribed texts of Irishness, how they relate (intertextually) to the external 'fixed' or accepted texts of Irishness, what role they might play in the horizontal intertextuality described above and how they might describe and appeal to Irish identities. As Barthes (1981a) points out, 'the intertext is a general field of anonymous formulae whose origin can scarcely ever be located; of unconscious or automatic quotations, given without the quotation marks' (p. 39). Thus, the objective is not to try and trace the textual roots of these advertisements to particular literary, historical texts, etc., but to see how such texts describe, and what role they play in, this horizontal intertextuality. A further aim is to go beyond the texts themselves, to assess how they 'explode and disperse' (Barthes 1981b: 135), how their fragments become part of this intertextual sphere to form new relationships with other texts and between texts and individuals.

Murphy's and the prescribed texts of Irish identity

The ad opens with a band singing 'The Wild Rover' at a wedding reception. The camera scans the scene to show a lecherous, if harmless, older man dancing with a younger woman who is fighting him off and a toothless (by implication simple and unworldly?) but respectful man dancing with another woman. We see the bride, the guests dancing and, finally, our hero, Murphy's Man, who stands, leaning against a wall, drinking a Murphy's and observing the scene in general and the bride in particular.

> Murphy's Man: 'I used to be an altar boy, with her brother' (indicates brother at the top table, kissing his sister, the bride, who playfully pushes him away).
>
> Murphy's Man and the bride make eye contact. 'I didn't always carry her books home from school', he smiles mischievously, "cause we didn't always go to school.' The bride blushes slightly, bows her head modestly, before looking up again to meet Murphy's Man's eyes, with more boldness this time. Murphy's Man becomes suddenly more serious and romantic: 'I was the first boy in Cork to kiss her.' The groom observes the scene suspiciously; the bride guiltily tries to reassure him.
>
> Murphy's Man: 'So, I suppose it should've been me. But like the Murphy's' (he takes a satisfying sip of Murphy's, observes the groom being pestered by the bride's mother and big brother and laughs) 'I'm not bitter.'
>
> He breaks into a smile and turns his attention to the bridesmaids.

Initially, the reading of this advertising text appears straightforward, its role in the intertextual construction of 'Irishness' and portrayal of Irish identity relatively simple. Intertextually, the story it tells feeds on the accepted texts of 'Irishness' and Irish identity as they have been read in Ireland, Britain and elsewhere. We hear echoes of the texts which document and perpetuate the stereotype of the happy, uncomplicated, flighty 'Paddy'[7] as hero. A given in such texts is the notion of the Irish as heavy drinkers and of alcohol forming the central focus of Irish social life. The images in the ad also sit comfortably with the texts of many British soap operas and their unchallenging portrayal of Irish characters (see Ingle 1996).

The musical text, the lyrics of the soundtrack, 'The Wild Rover' (the prototypical Irish ballad about the stereotypical flighty Irish rogue), form a core part of the intertextual sphere. The groom's days as a wild rover are over now that he has been caught in the clutches of the stereotypical Irish woman and her mother, with only marriage on their minds. In this we can hear echoes of dramatic texts such as the plays of John B. Keane.[8] Murphy's Man, on the other hand, has had a lucky escape (the assumed aim of all Irish men) and is free to play the wild rover for a little while longer.

The other fixed texts of 'Irishness' are also present in the ad: the altar-boy reference (which calls up the religious texts and the textual depiction of Ireland as a priest-ridden country where all men were originally altar boys); the interfering Irish mother; the craic[9] at the wedding; the textual writing of Ireland as a patriarchal society. Intertextually, this links to the other Murphy's ads in the series, in which the atmosphere is male – the role of unmarried women being downplayed. Here we see it in the form of the blushing, virginal Irish bride. This advertising text is a timeless picture of a country untouched by the sophistication of modern life. It is the 'old Ireland', a snapshot which could have been taken any time over the last forty years and which observes the intertextual hierarchy discussed above. The sacred place of the family in Irish life, for example, as laid down in the Constitution and other foundational texts and made official by the texts of the Church, schools, etc., is brought into every-day reality in the text of this Irish wedding. However, the strictly controlled morality of Irish society should never be read at a surface level. Is the bride really the blushing virgin? Is she worried about the choice she has made? What have the bridesmaids got in mind? The surface reading, using the prescribed texts of Irish identity, does not penetrate through to the writings at the individual level – the subversion and stretching of these prescribed texts and the ability to pursue an entirely contradictory existence while living within them. The assumption of the strict intertextual hierarchy of foundational, official and everyday texts ignores this reality.

Some insight into the origin of the ad reveals the superficiality of such a reading. One of the aims of the campaign for Murphy's was to challenge the dominance of Guinness in the stout market. Guinness forms the omnipresent intertext, both indirectly (as discussed above) and also directly, since the Murphy's slogan 'I'm not bitter' is a direct reference to the rival stout, considered less sweet than Murphy's. The adverts themselves are the product of London agency Bartle Bogle Hagarty, and the first series (of which this ad is a part) was directed by Alan Parker, having taken his inspiration from *The Commitments*.[10] Interestingly, the latest series is directed by Declan Lowney, responsible for the Irish comedy show *Father Ted* (Marshall 1997a). Thus, the two directors form an interesting intertextual link with the cinematic text of *The Commitments* and the wacky humour of *Father Ted*. Furthermore, the ads were shown predominantly on the non-mainstream Channel 4 on Friday and Saturday evenings in the commercial breaks during programmes such as American comedy *Frasier* and *Father Ted*. The latter, in particular, not only forms the co-text but also part of the intertextual sphere within which the Murphy's campaign functions. *Father Ted* can also be accepted through a superficial reading as deriding the Catholic stereotype and the institution of the Church in Ireland. However, here again the writing of other texts onto this picture reveals much more. In these texts we see the ability and confidence to take possession of and in the process exploit one's own stereotype, while at the same time recognizing that one can take on elements of that identity as desired or as the situation arises.

Here we can see how, through new intertextual relations, a basically very negative stereotype, the drunken 'Paddy', which has both contributed to and resulted from the textual depiction of the Irish 'as a group who are lacking in intelligence, drunken, stupid, lazy, untamed, requiring civilisation, dirty, wild and inherently prone to violence' (Taylor 1992: 6) in Britain, has in fact become the central source text for the positive commercial texts of 'Irishness', most notably in the texts of the Irish pub. These advertising texts depend on the reconstitution of the negative 'Paddy' texts and their 'grafting', as Barthes terms it, on to the texts of literature, music, mysticism and *craic* through the texts of, among others, Guinness and the Irish pub. Through this intertextual linking, 'Paddy' (here Murphy's Man) has become the most attractive man in Europe – roguish, mysterious, deep and romantic.

What is also important in this intertextual construction is not only the texts that are used, but who uses them and how they are used – who is doing the writing, and who is seen to do the writing. If the stereotype is used – or, perhaps more accurately, seen to be used – by the objects of that stereotype, then they are no longer reading what others have written about them, but are in fact writing it themselves. In other words, because these texts are being used, being written by and for an 'Irish' product, they can, perhaps, validly or more validly be used in the construction of an Irish identity. Furthermore, Murphy's Man does not seem too bothered about his stereotype or how it will be read – it is one which he seems able to adopt as the mood takes him – and there is a certain detachment about him and his knowledge of this along with his ability to write his own identity text.

Contradictions abound in the ad and in the product itself – as in the construction of a hybridized and complex identity (cf. Smith 1991). Murphy's brewery, for instance, is located in Cork, hence the mention of the city in the ad (in fact all of the Murphy's ads show landmarks of either the city or the coastline). However, our hero, far from having the distinctive Cork accent, seems to hail from a northern county – perhaps Cavan or Monaghan. This is unlikely to be an oversight on the part of the advertisers and should not be regarded as a lapse in authenticity. Murphy's Man is the composite Irish man, the product of numerous commercial texts, acceptable in Ireland and elsewhere.[11]

Kilkenny and the texts of the emerald tiger

In this advertisement young people talk about their first kiss through a collage of incomplete sentences and statements. The background imagery presents images of childhood and nostalgia for childhood – the fairground, amusements, cartoon characters – alongside images of teenage romance – lipstick, butterflies, picking petals from a flower. The overwhelming feeling of the advertising text is of innocent sophistication:

> 'My first real kiss?'
> 'Yeah.'
> 'I remember thinkin' –'
> 'Those first few seconds –'
> 'I didn't want it to end.'
> 'Was I stunned?'
> 'I was stunned!'
> 'A tad scary –'
> 'It's more than just the lips and tongue.'
> 'It's ecstasy.'
> 'It's who you're with.'
> 'Where you are –'
> 'Wow!'
> 'Well worth the wait.'
> 'I felt all kind of tingly.'
> 'I remember thinking –'
> 'Bullseye!'
> 'The buzz going everywhere –'
> 'I thought I'd never get over it.'
> 'It's one of those things you get better at all the time.'
> 'Yeah, I'd say I'm pretty good at it.'
> ''Cause you never forget your first kiss.'

The Kilkenny ad stands in stark contrast to the one for Murphy's. Kilkenny was developed by Guinness and, after being successfully marketed in Germany, the beer was introduced to Britain. Interestingly, the advertising agency responsible for the campaign, the London-based Publicis, started the advertising campaign in Hamburg – the popularity of Irish pubs in the north German city being the reason behind this (Campaign 1996). Given the Guinness connection, it might seem obvious that Kilkenny would use Guinness texts as an intertextual 'support'. However, the Kilkenny approach is very different and its texts work in conjunction with a different range of texts.

The ad is very much a text of the 'new Ireland' and relies on the intertextual sphere of the 'emerald tiger' and Mary Robinson's[12] presidency. For example, the following extracts show how economic texts dealing with Ireland have changed:

> For many years, the Republic of Ireland was referred to in the same breath with countries such as Greece, Portugal and Spain – EU members whose standards of living continually fell way below the average of their European partners. This is no longer the case. (Institut der Deutschen Wirtschaft 1996)

> Which country in the European Union is enjoying an economic boom, Germany or Ireland? Take your time … British economic machismo, already much dented by relative decline, is facing a new and unpalatable truth … the 'emerald tiger' is surpassing Britain in growth and income per head. (Kemp 1997)

These examples acknowledge the changing intertextual sphere within which notions of Ireland and 'Irishness' are evaluated. It is within this new sphere that the Kilkenny ad has meaning.

Self-confident, attractive, articulate, educated, young Irish people – identifiable principally through their accents – talk about the experience of their first kiss and, by implication, their first Kilkenny. The young people in the ad seem worlds away from the gauche, quirky Murphy's Man. The images in the ad are non-culture-specific and, rather than using traditional music or ballads, the ad is set to a blues soundtrack. In contrast to the Murphy's text, women play an equal role in the Kilkenny ad. These are 'cool' Irish people who believe that they belong to one of the 'trendiest' cultures in Europe. Here we see links with the promotional texts produced by the Irish Industrial Development Authority on the theme 'The Young Europeans',[13] and, in fact, the identity presented here is very much rooted in the European context, which has provided so much of the background to the writing of these new texts of 'Irishness'. Ironically, it is membership of the pan-national European Union that has perhaps done most to develop a positive sense of national identity; it has offered the possibility of defining the identity as something other than 'not English'.

However, here and there the older texts show through. The slogan 'Kiss the Kilkenny' alludes to the tradition of kissing the Blarney Stone, which is supposed to transmit to the kisser the famous Irish 'gift of the gab' or ability to talk. This story, widely exploited in tourist texts, also forms an intertextual link with other non-commercial texts, as the following quote from an article on Irish swimmer Michelle Smith illustrates: 'It took a fair degree of blarney to get her reinstated after an appeal' (Hodgson 1996). The notion of the Irish as romantics, deep thinkers and poets is also alluded to, particularly in the form of the final young man, who expresses himself in a slow, contemplative and pseudo-intellectual way in which advertisers would never try to portray a young English person, particularly in a text advertising an alcoholic product.[14]

Thus, we see what Luke Gibbons (1996) has referred to as the cultural schizophrenia in the marketing texts of 'Irishness'. On the one hand, the Irish economy is now highly developed and in many ways more advanced than its European counterparts, having to a large extent missed out on the heavy-industry era to end up a leading player in the information-technology sector. This is the image promoted by the government and industrialists. On the other hand, the tourist industry continues to project an image of an under-developed, unspoilt country with a slow pace of life. It is only recently that the agencies concerned have realized that such apparently contradictory images can in fact be married together and accommodated successfully in promotional texts, as in the case of Kilkenny. A comment made during the 1997 Eurovision Song Contest broadcast from Dublin sums up the new approach: Ireland is being promoted in such texts as the land of 'computers and culture'.

Caffrey's and the texts of the diasporic and fractured community

The ad begins with four 'cool', sophisticated 'guys' walking playfully down the streets of New York and into an Irish bar, then moves between their game of pool and snatches of conversation in other parts of the bar. The conversation at the pool table switches to television, one of the friends saying, with an American accent, 'The power of television is an amazing thing. I didn't cry as hard when my dog died as when Henry died on *Mash*.' Again, we hear echoes of the shared texts of that generation's identity, which are not limited to the prescribed hierarchy – *Mash* being of course an American series. His friend retorts playfully with an Irish accent, 'Shut up there boys, I'm trying to play pool.' All around the pub there are stereotypical images of (American) 'Irishness' – posters, flags etc. The pounding backing track is the House of Pain's song 'Jump'.

Then the pool player orders a Caffrey's – 'Can I have a Caffrey's please there' – and as he waits for the beer to settle in the glass, the scene is transported to the emerald isle in an unashamed overdose of nostalgia. There follows image after image of a sepia Ireland: the rushing clouds, the comely, red-haired maiden (alluring but decent), the hurling team led by the parish priest, the quiet men in the pub whom time has forgotten. We hear echoes of many other texts here, the commercial espousal of the beautiful landscape and a certain quaint backwardness and the urban horses and cowboys of cinematic texts such as *The Commitments* and *Into the West*.[15] The musical background to this part of the ad, from the soundtrack of *Miller's Crossing* (a film about Irish-American gangsters), is reminiscent of Irish nationalist composer Sean O'Riada's suite *Mise Éire*.[16] This piece was itself instrumental in constructing 'Irishness' and promoting cultural and national pride. Finally, we return to the boys in the New York bar as they drink their Caffrey's and look meaningfully, deeply into the camera, and we see the slogan, 'Strong words softly spoken'.

Caffrey's was invented by British brewers Bass in 1994 to target 'the ageing lager drinker … looking for a mature pint' (Armstrong 1996). The drink itself, the product launch and the advertising campaign have all been the subject of praise; Caffrey's represents 'a triumph of beer marketing' (Armstrong 1996). The brand's three main features – and the basis for the advertising campaign – are described by the Bass sales director as 'its unconventionality, its exuberance and, above all, its Irish provenance' (Watkins 1995).

The Caffrey's advertising text itself has generated other media texts discussing 'Irishness' and Irish identities. For example,

Douglas Kennedy made the following analysis in the *Sunday Times*:[17]

> A sip of this frothy drink will immediately transport you out of some yob-festooned New York bar and back to a realm of Celtic enchantment: a place where all hills are green, where all mist is misht, and where a wind-swept maiden with flaming red hair is guaranteed to fix you with her dewy-eyed stare. (Kennedy 1996)

It could be argued, however, that Kennedy is missing the point. The ad takes place in what is clearly an Irish pub; the 'yobs' are actually dancing to the music of Irish-American hip-hop band House of Pain. The four friends in the ad are a far cry from the maudlin emigrants of earlier times. They are smiling, exuding an air of confidence. Kennedy criticizes the ad for not transporting the hero back to the complexity that is modern Ireland. His criticism, however, shows a total misunderstanding of the emigrant experience and, in fact, of how Irish identity is read and written. The emigrant rarely yearns for the reality of his previous existence, but looks instead to just such idealized images and texts. The ad and the images it portrays are unashamedly nostalgic and never attempt or pretend to be realistic. It is explicit in its use of an over-the-top collage of Irish cultural icons.

Nostalgia has been one of the key factors of a diasporic Irish identity since the nineteenth century. Emigrants mourn for a country they may not have consciously loved or which may not even have interested them when they lived there (cf. O'Toole 1997a: 134–5). With geographical and temporal distance, however, 'traditions of myth and music can be explored again with a new-found and non-fanatical freedom' (Kearney 1988: 186). As Smith (1991) points out, it is mythical attachments and associations rather than actual residence (or even citizenship) that are key here. In fact one of the aims of London advertising agency WCRS, which was responsible for the campaign, was 'to combine sentimentality about one's roots with a gregarious contemporary optimism ... the drinker returns to the bar from his old Ireland thoughts with a new perspective'. Interestingly, they also comment that 'it's not an image British drinkers will associate with their own beers, but it is possible to attach emotional imagery to Ireland' (Armstrong 1996).

Furthermore, the Irish pub is frequented by a mixture of other identities – it is something inclusive, not something to be jealously protected and strictly defined through the hierarchical process. It benefits from dilution and hybridity – just as House of Pain uses rap and hip-hop music, rather than traditional Irish forms, to express the second-generation emigrant experience. The ad's text also gives validity, not only to the Irish emigrant experience, but also to the experience of the second-generation Irish and their need to express that particular aspect of their identity. In this, the ad has meaning within the intertextual sphere of films such as *The Brothers McMullen*, in which the lives of three Irish-American brothers are explored.

There are also echoes of the texts of and about Irish president Mary Robinson.[18] As O'Toole (1997b) observes, '[Mary Robinson] has made herself head of a state that has no formal, institutional existence – a state that includes the Irish diaspora in the US, Britain and around the world, that includes the grief of Northern Ireland' (O'Toole 1997b). Thus, she has in effect promoted the notion of the cultural, diasporic nation and this advertising text is both a product and a source of such an identity. Rather than being portrayed as 'plastic paddies' – the pejorative term for second-generation Irish, as if they are in some way inferior to the real product – the hero's friends (despite their American accents) have access to the experience of 'Irishness' through, for example, commercial texts.

So too do those living in Northern Ireland, and this other sore point of 'Irishness' is also touched on in the ad, albeit indirectly. Caffrey's is brewed in Northern Ireland, in County Antrim (perceived as one of the most staunchly 'Protestant' counties in Northern Ireland). However, the identity suggested by the ad and the product are undeniably 'Irish' – not in any political or religious sense, but in what could be termed a Celtic sense. Equally, the experience of emigration which forms part of the intertextual sphere of the advertisement is one that has affected all parts of the island. Interestingly, Caffrey's chose nostalgia for Belfast's shipyards as the theme of its second ad – thus making an explicit link with Northern Ireland and its texts.

A key feature of this and other Irish marketing texts is that they are rather inclusive in their definition of 'Irishness'; they seek to link texts defining culture and identity, at a level that precludes or even nullifies the political and sectarian text. For example, Guinness makes the following statement: 'From a population of five million, the island of Ireland has produced an astonishing number of artists who have achieved fame, fortune and critical acclaim on the international music stage' (Guinness, no date). At first glance the statement seems harmless and uncontested. However, no politician would risk the controversial assertion that the population of 'Ireland' is 'five million' – the sum of Northern Ireland (1.5 million) and the Republic (3.5 million). As Roy Foster rightly points out, in political and journalistic texts relating to politics, '"Ireland" is employed to refer indiscriminately to Northern Ireland and/or the Republic, in a way that sets teeth on edge on both sides of the border' (Foster 1996). However, the use of 'Ireland' in the cultural/commercial text is uncontested. Such texts instead map out other identities, ignoring the texts which should provide the obvious or prescribed links.

The cultural nation of the marketing text thus overrides political boundaries, sectarian divides, religion and citizenship. The citizen of Northern Ireland who may define him/herself as unionist does not boycott Guinness and Riverdance in favour of stereotypically British cultural products. When they go to Britain, many are more likely to define themselves as Irish and do not feel that they compromise their political or community affinities when they visit an Irish pub. Interestingly, this notion of Irish identity harks back to a Yeatsian myth of a unifying Celtic identity for the island that would 'provide the segregated Irish people with a common currency of "holy symbols" ... a memory beyond all individual memories' (Kearney 1997: 114). And, today, in the texts of commodified Irish culture, we see too a common currency of marketed symbols which forge and maintain, through a variety of intertextual links, what are both intangible and yet very powerful bonds and markers of a shared identity.

Take, for example, the following marketing text, which ignores the texts defining the geopolitics of the Northern Ireland conflict, thus ignoring too the prescribed intertextual route, the hierarchy of foundational, official and unofficial:

> One of Ireland's greatest treasures is the abundance of clean, clear waters. Many of these great waterways are concentrated in an area that we like to call Ireland's Unspoilt Angling Waters ... The area stretches from Loch Gowna in County Cavan across green rolling hills north to Dungannon in County Tyrone, embracing an area east to Carrickmacross in County Monaghan, along meandering rivers, up fast flowing streams and west over deep and tranquil

> lakelands towards Belleek in County Fermanagh and on to lovely Leitrim. (Fermanagh District Council *et al.*, no date)

In this brief text we have in fact criss-crossed the border between Northern Ireland and the Republic; the text's assortment of counties form part of two different states in political texts.

In the rest of the brochure we see the links with other texts of 'Irishness' and the key aspects of that identity, which are written as applying to all areas of Ireland, regardless of geography, religion or political affiliations:

> As well as the peaceful unspoilt countryside, there are friendly villages and towns with cosy, old fashioned pubs where a warm welcome awaits after a rewarding day on the water. Entertainment comes naturally … You'll quickly feel at home among these hospitable folks. (Fermanagh District Council *et al.*, no date)

It is only with the note at the end of the brochure that the political and administrative text interrupts this Celtic utopia, by prescribing the geopolitical boundaries and making an explicit link with the prescribed structure of official texts: 'Contact any Irish or Northern Ireland Tourist Board office.'

Conclusion

By choosing at will from historical narratives, folk memories, foundational texts and their myths, the official texts of institutions and also economic, journalistic and cinematic texts from a variety of domestic and international sources, these advertising texts illustrate how 'Irishness' and Irish identity today are no longer constituted through the prescribed intertextual hierarchy of the past. Instead these are gleaned from a constantly changing plethora of global and national offerings, the strength of the mixture changing from situation to situation and from individual to individual. It is the refusal of uniformity and a standard reading of the texts of Irish culture and identity, demanding instead that such identity be constantly written and rewritten anew. The choices made in these advertising texts – as with individual experiences – reflect contradictions and inconsistencies, nostalgia and realism, and the intertextual sphere within which they operate and have meaning is itself subject to constantly shifting borders and changing parameters.[19]

Ironically, despite the apparent simplicity of the hierarchical construct and the notion of vertical intertextuality, the horizontal intertextuality which has largely replaced this is in many ways less complicated, more honest, at least at the level of the intertextual process of our everyday lives.

The introduction of these commercial and advertising texts of 'Irishness' into the intertextual sphere has added something to the construction of Irish identity. For example, it could be argued that the promotional and commercial texts have, to a certain extent, depoliticized the expression of the identity in the UK; the presence of such texts dilutes the image and challenges the accepted and fixed texts. The act of visiting the Irish pub and enjoying its texts today is not a political statement, as it was twenty years ago; it no longer means that the individual subscribes to the old hierarchy and the prescribed texts that ordain the nature of the relationship between the Republic of Ireland, Northern Ireland and Britain. The inclusion of the diasporic experience in these advertising texts and their disregard for political, economic and social realities also illustrate that these texts and intertextual relationships render the question of authenticity largely irrelevant.

Finally, it can be argued that the advertising and commercial texts have now somewhat depressingly, but perhaps predictably, come to compose the new prescribed texts of 'Irishness' and may eventually become the foundational texts, forming the givens and providing the pathways through which new texts of 'Irishness' will in turn be read and written.

Notes

1   The relationship with the Irish language too and the texts dealing with it have come to acknowledge the contradictory situation whereby in the 1991 Census almost one third of the population reported that they could speak Irish, despite the reality of the average Irish person's lack of proficiency in the language. As John Edwards points out, the language, having lost its communicative function, does however continue 'to serve a symbolic function for many' (Edwards 1985: 64). What for the majority was a tokenistic relationship has only recently been acknowledged and this changes the prescribed hierarchy of the key role of Irish as laid down in foundational texts. This prescription of Irish as the first language in the Constitution prescribed in turn the presumed (albeit aspirational) role for the language in everyday life, education, etc.

2   The issue of Northern Ireland is dealt with in greater detail below (pp. 36ff.).

3   For instance in the writing of Joe Lee, Fintan O'Toole, Luke Gibbons, Richard Kearney, Declan Kiberd, Dermot Bolger, Roddy Doyle, Glen

Patterson, Joe O'Connor.

4   Cf., for instance, *The Barrytown Trilogy*, *Paddy Clarke, Ha, Ha, Ha* or *The Woman who Walked into Doors*.

5   Heinrich Böll's *Irisches Tagebuch* or *Irish Diary*, written in the 1950s, has become the key text in the Hiberno-German relationship and forms the basis for many Germans' 'love affair' with the island.

6   My emphasis and translation.

7   Pejorative term for Irish, derivative of common Irish first name, Patrick.

8   John B. Keane, playwright, author and chronicler of small-town, rural Ireland. Most notably in plays such as *Big Maggie* (an exploration of a dominating and manipulative Irish mother) and *The Field* (produced as a film by Noel Pearson in 1990) he has been able to explore the Irish condition and to present the audience with the subtext beneath the orderly surface.

9   Irish (Gaelic) word for fun and merriment used in everyday Irish English.

10 See note 15.

11 Further contradictions appear when we investigate who is in fact writing these texts. Murphy's is distributed and marketed by Whitbread in the UK, a major player in the food and drink sector with a very different corporate image to Murphy's brewery in Ladywell, Cork. The company is also responsible for such diverse brand identities as Labatts (the advertising for which uses the mounty police to emphasize its Canadian credentials), Stella Artois (identified as continental, francophone Belgian) and the Euro-beer Heineken. The advertising team at Bartley Bogle Hegarty responsible for the Murphy's ad is also charged with creating advertising texts for Boddington's (exploiting a strong Manchester identity) and the Australian Rolling Rock. The agency was also given the task of advertising Murphy's in Ireland and devised an off-the-wall campaign featuring a group of Samurai warriors, which resulted in much discussion and a cult following in Ireland (Marshall 1997b). As one commentator noted, 'while young British pub society has become saturated with emeraldisle ersatz, its counterpart in the real Ireland is consigning such things to the past' (Hill 1997).

12 Discussed in more detail below (pp. 36ff.). See also note 18.

13 The promotional literature and billboard posters presented Ireland's young, educated population as its greatest economic resource.

14 It is, however, important to note that the presentation could be applied to a Scottish or even a Welsh young person.

15 *The Commitments*, Alan Parker's 1991 film version of the Roddy Doyle novel, tells the story of a group of Dublin youths who 'believing that the Irish are the blacks of Europe, form a soul band' (Walker 1995). *Into the West*, a 1992 production, relates events involving two young boys from a family of settled travellers who run away from home on their magical white horse, Tír na nÓg ('Land of the young' – in Irish mythology a place of eternal youth to which Oisin travelled on his white horse). Both stories feature the urban experience of poverty in Ireland and present aspects of that culture which would previously have been deemed too shameful to be the subject of a cultural product, such as youths riding horses around estates in Dublin and other major cities or the position of the travelling community in Irish life.

16 In English 'I am Ireland'. The music was commissioned as the soundtrack to a documentary of the same name.

17 The title page of the supplement 'The Culture' contained the image of a laughing leprechaun sitting on a giant shamrock and sipping a frothy drink against a backdrop of green hills. The heading read 'BLARNEY! Falling for the myth of the Emerald Isle'.

18 Cf., for example, Mary Robinson's inaugural speech of 3 December 1990.

19 This was illustrated by a *Daily Telegraph* report of a recent study by the Commission for Racial Equality on discrimination against the Irish community in Britain. The article was not the only text in that particular edition to deal with Irishness. An anti-IRA editorial and several reports dealt with Irish terrorists. A text on the back page contained a condescending report about a quaint occurrence in a small Irish town. The economic pages detailed the positive financial performance of the country. Finally, yet another text dealt with a very different aspect of Irish identity: the cultural phenomenon of the band U2 and their universal popularity.

References and bibliography

Anderson, B. (1981), *Imagined Communities*, London: Verso.

Armstrong, S. (1996), 'Can advertising win the beer war?', *Campaign*, 14 June, 32.

Barthes, R. (1981a), 'Theory of the text', in R. Young (ed.), *Untying the Text: A Poststructuralist Reader*, London: Routledge & Kegan Paul.

Barthes, R. (1981b), 'Textual analysis of Poe's Valdemar', in R. Young (ed.), *Untying the Text: A Post-structuralist Reader*, London: Routledge & Kegan Paul.

Billig, M. (1995), *Banal Nationalism*, London: Sage.

Campaign (1996), *Guinness appoints Publicis London to run pan-Euro push*, *Campaign*, 27 September, 2.

Carty, C. (1996), 'The Irish Cultural Road Show comes to town', *Sunday Tribune Magazine*, 6 December, 29.

Edwards, J. (1985), *Language, Society and Identity*, Oxford: Blackwell in association with André Deutsch.

Fermanagh District Council, Dungannon District Council, North West Regional Tourism Organisation (no date), *Ireland's Unspoilt Angling Waters: Cavan. Fermanagh. Leitrim. Monaghan. South Tyrone.*

Foster, R. (1996), 'Ireland's English troubles', *Observer Review*, 18 February, 4.

Gibbons, L. (1996), *Transformations in Irish Culture*, Cork: Cork University Press.

Green, A. (1996), 'Can O & M produce another winner for Guinness?', *Campaign*, 8 March, 12.

Guinness (1996), *Guinness Irish Pub Concept*, London and Dublin: Guinness Brewing Worldwide (internal publication).

Guinness (no date), *The Guinness Irish Pub: It's Time to Open*, London and Dublin: Guinness Brewing Worldwide.

Hill, D. (1997) 'Stout louder', *Observer*, 11 May, 8.

Hobsbawm, E. (1990), *Nations and Nationalism since 1780: Programme, Myth, Reality*, Cambridge: Cambridge University Press.

Hodgson, G. (1996), 'Smith's gold makes Irish history', *Independent (Sport)*, 22 July, S24.

Hussey, G. (1995), *Ireland Today: Anatomy of a Changing State*, Harmondsworth: Penguin.

Ingle, R. (1996), 'TV soaps savour mad, bad Irish', *Sunday Tribune*, 10 March, 7.

Institut der Deutschen Wirtschaft (1996), 'Grune Insel unter Euro-Dampf', *IWD*, 49, 5 December, 7.

Irish Tourist Board (1996a), *Irland: Europas grune Ferieninsel*.

Irish Tourist Board (1996b), *Ireland: A Romantic Blend*.

James, P. (1996), *Nation Formation: Towards a Theory of Abstract Community*, London: Sage.

Kearney, R. (1988), *Transitions: Narratives in Modern Irish Culture*, Manchester: Manchester University Press.

Kearney, R. (1997), *Postnationalist Ireland: Politics, Culture, Philosophy*, London: Routledge.

Kemp, A. (1997), '"Emerald Tiger" has last laugh', *Observer*, 2 February, 24.

Kennedy, D. (1996), 'Where the grass is always greener', *The Sunday Times* (The Culture), 10 November, 10.4–10.5.

Kiberd, D. (1996), *Inventing Ireland: The Literature of the Modern Nation*, London: Vintage.

Lee, J. J. (1989), *Ireland 1912–1985: Politics and Society*, Cambridge: Cambridge University Press.

Marshall, C. (1997a), 'BBH uses Fr. Ted director for Murphy's', *Campaign*, 7 March, 7.

Marshall, C. (1997b), 'BBH uses kung fu for Irish Murphy's', *Campaign*, 2 May, 6.

O'Connor, J. (1994), *The Secret World of the Irish Male*, Dublin: New Island Books.

O'Toole, F. (1997a), *The Ex-Isle of Erin: Images of a Global Ireland*, Dublin: New Island Books.

O'Toole, F. (1997b), 'No politician in the history of the State has commanded such respect and popularity', *The Irish Times*, 13 March, 6.

Smith, A. D. (1991), *National Identity*, Harmondsworth: Penguin.

Stena Line (1997), *Holiday Ireland*.

Taylor, S. (1992), 'The Irish in Britain – an ethnic minority community experiencing disadvantage and discrimination – the implications for Birmingham City Council's equal opportunities practice', Text of a speech given to the Irish Community Consultative Conference, Birmingham City Council, 1 November.

Thomas Cook (1997), *Thomas Cook Holidays: Ireland*.

Walker, J. (1995), *Haliwell's Film Guide*, 11th edn, London: HarperCollins.

Waters, J. (1991), *Jiving at the Crossroads*, Belfast: Blackstaff Press.

Watkins, S. (1995), 'WCRS unveils Bass ale film', *Campaign*, 12 May.

3

Spitting Image: TV genre and intertextuality

ULRIKE H. MEINHOF AND JONATHAN SMITH

Spitting Image: political satire or television pastiche?

In this chapter we offer some reflections on a British television programme of the late 1980s and early 1990s. Almost exactly a decade elapsed between the first series of *Spitting Image*, broadcast in 1984, and a much-publicized 'final' one that has been followed only by brief and half-hearted come-backs. During this time the programme achieved a level of popularity with a sufficiently broad audience to amount almost to a cult.

Beginning in 1987, special editions of *Spitting Image* were broadcast nationwide (but on commercial channels which in Britain are organized on a regional basis) in a special slot scheduled immediately before the one carrying live general-election results. This is a clear indication of the programme's prestige with programmers, advertisers and the general audience. However, contrary to what the timing of these special editions might seem to suggest (in common with a considerable amount of other commentary), we shall argue that its appeal by no means depended solely on its being used or perceived as a vehicle of political satire. Instead, we suggest that at least during some stages of its history, *Spitting Image*'s appeal, and indeed its comprehensibility, depended equally (and perhaps to an even greater extent) on viewers' familiarity with British television in general. Referring to material from the early 1990s, we show how parody of an extensive range of TV programming, and not just of political television or even politics, had by that time come to be a principal feature of *Spitting Image*. This also means that the programme is a prime candidate for intertextual study of an illustrative kind.

We would not, however, wish to suggest that our remarks here exhaust what might be said about ways in which *Spitting Image* communicated with its audience. Remarkably, a proportion of the original programmes were re-broadcast in Germany, where they also inspired an imitator-series, *Hurra Deutschland!* ('Hurray for Germany!'), as they have elsewhere, and most recently in Israel (*Hartzufim*, a title that has been translated into colloquial English as 'Crappy Cheeky Faces'). However, the various different kinds of sense that German, Israeli and other international audiences may have been able to make of either kind of programme exceed the scope of the present discussion. Another initial qualification of what we say below is suggested by Wagg (1992: 276), who gives an account of divisions among those responsible for producing the programme in its early years, between those who saw it as light entertainment and those who aspired to political satire.

As we shall see, the programme was a topic of controversy in the media, as it was more widely. On occasion it stood accused of contributing to the degradation of political life, even to the extent of distorting electoral behaviour through cheap and vulgar caricature of allegedly serious politicians. However, such suggestions that *Spitting Image* had real effects on the political process in its narrow definition fail entirely to recognize the generic nature of this programme, which we shall define by the term 'TV pastiche'. They also take a simplistic view of audiences' responses to television in general, conceiving them as simple 'effects' of a single immediate 'cause' in much the same way that the depiction of violence on television is sometimes held to 'cause' rising crime rates in society at large (see Masterman 1994 for a sophisticated but introductory discussion of the media and society that consistently problematizes the relationship between them and surveys a good deal of recent research). Moreover, the conflation of politics and entertainment to be found in *Spitting Image* reflects something which has in any case been much more widely observed and is expressed in commonplace neologisms such as 'infotainment' (or 'conversationalization' – see Fairclough 1995). Our description of *Spitting Image*'s generic format will therefore illustrate this more general process, as well as tentatively suggesting a more nuanced conception of the relationship between the programme and the political process.

ULRIKE H. MEINHOF AND JONATHAN SMITH

Visual intertextuality: spitting puppets

One thing in particular distinguished this television programme from all others, namely its grotesque, life-size, latex puppets of well-known figures and characters, both fictional and real. These puppets' sole common denominator was the great familiarity their originals had already previously gained from media exposure, principally on TV. This meant that the puppets were instantaneously recognizable to the generality of viewers, despite the frequently immense exaggeration of particular aspects of a figure's physiognomy, physique, behaviour, dress or character. One such trait would frequently be used to make metaphorical reference to another. Prime Minister John Major, for example, was consistently shown dressed in grey and grey in the face, as a sign of boredom, dullness and lack of energy. Similarly, the various successive puppets representing his predecessor Margaret Thatcher were characterized by an increasingly aggressive demeanour and accessories, and tended to be depicted in settings that were ever more macabre: towards the end of her time in office, this led to her being depicted as a mad butcher engaged in slaughtering with a cleaver the queues of jobless at her (Job Centre) office door. In this way, selected properties of individual puppets were made to stand as comments on the personalities of the figures they depicted, and in some cases on their activities in public life.

This process was both more complex and more varied than the foregoing examples might seem to suggest. For instance, the idea of David Owen's domination of David Steel during the period of the alliance between their respective Social Democrat and Liberal parties was conveyed by a gross disproportion in the size of their puppets. Steel could sit in Owen's pocket, and on occasion he literally did so. However, comparable elements of absurdity also crept in where no political message was involved. For instance, in contrast to common perceptions of her staid demeanour the Queen Mother featured as a rocking granny in pink lycra leggings. The success of the puppets was such that by the early 1990s they had begun to appear elsewhere, substituting in the press and other television programmes for their originals when these were to be targets for the type of semi-satirical and semi-gratuitous humour we have exemplified. Thus in 1996 the Labour Party used a *Spitting Image*-style puppet of John Major in a party political broadcast showing him

45

clutching a lifebelt bearing the word *Titanic* – an intertextual reference to the stereotype of a captain too proud to heed warnings of danger ahead. It is one measure of the degree to which the puppets captured the public imagination that they have continued to enjoy a twilit half-life in this type of context since regular series of *Spitting Image* ceased being broadcast. Another is that they also came to be objects of interest in their own right: in the early 1990s a *Spitting Image* Museum in London displayed the puppets to the public in much the same way waxworks are displayed at Madame Tussaud's.

The high proportion of political figures among the puppets might seem to suggest that *Spitting Image* was primarily a vehicle for political satire, and we shall consider some arguments to this effect below. However, arguments of this type do not in themselves tell us much about what distinguished *Spitting Image* from other forms of political satire; nor do they tell us anything about what it had in common with other TV programmes. These are serious issues from the point of view of media studies, because *Spitting Image* consists of TV pastiche or parody quite as much as in anything else. This pastiche or parody takes as its object or target not simply individual TV programmes, but also the more anonymous and generalized generic formats of television programmes and, occasionally, a sequence of such formats which combine to parody an entire evening's schedule. This is a part of what makes *Spitting Image* an obvious candidate for study in the context of a book of this kind: the programme made unusually explicit a certain kind of otherwise largely unformalized knowledge of the ways in which meanings are produced and exchanged, by programme makers and by their audiences.

Before illustrating this point in detail, we shall first show how this pattern of specifically televisual intertextuality is largely occluded in one particular discussion of *Spitting Image* where the programme is classified as political satire. This is all the more striking as the discussion in question itself takes the form of a television programme. Dating from the winter of 1990 and therefore from around the time when *Spitting Image* was at the peak of its notoriety, it is an episode of the *South Bank Show*, London Weekend Television's prestigious cultural review programme, which continues to be broadcast nationwide, regularly and during peak viewing time, on Sunday evenings. It is to a discussion of this *South Bank Show* programme that we now turn.

ULRIKE H. MEINHOF AND JONATHAN SMITH

Spitting Image and the *South Bank Show*

Spitting Image is described both by the presenter of the *South Bank Show*, Melvyn Bragg, and by the then deputy leader of the Labour Party, Roy Hattersley, as continuing a tradition of British political satire exemplified by the eighteenth- and early nineteenth-century painters and draughtsmen Hogarth, Gillray and Rowlandson. While this aestheticist identification of *Spitting Image* with satirical drawings and etchings of previous centuries may have some force, it nevertheless obscures the fundamental difference between the genres in question.

Once the possibility is raised that *Spitting Image* might be understood in this way, as being a relatively traditional kind of political satire, a debate about its merits relative to earlier examples of the tradition necessarily obscures from then onwards the point – which in our view is a crucial one – that *Spitting Image* is primarily about television. Rather than registering this, the *South Bank Show* programme accumulates the different opinions of various politicians, journalists and broadcasters on the supposedly central question of *Spitting Image*'s function in the context of the political process as they (somewhat narrowly) define it. This question itself is also very substantially clouded by the way discussion of it is interspersed with a continuing, and logically distinct, argument about the justice or otherwise of re-classifying *Spitting Image* as part of a venerable cultural tradition. In the course of this discussion, other participants in the programme suggest less honorific descriptions of *Spitting Image* than those proposed by Bragg and Hattersley: it is variously dismissed as being 'just a load of fictions', 'just school-boy humour', 'only telly', 'not important', 'popular mass entertainment' and a cartoon comparable to Bugs Bunny.

In this vein, eminent figures mount a series of counter-attacks on *Spitting Image* which are all apparently rooted in contempt for contemporary popular culture. The Bragg–Hattersley project of re-casting the programme as political satire counteracts this kind of association by placing it in a long-standing national tradition. Other commentators are less complimentary. Thus the well-known current affairs broadcaster Robin Day angrily contends that *Spitting Image* is 'biased against democracy and reasonable behaviour'. The *Times* journalist Barbara Amiel takes a line similar to Day's: *Spitting Image* has taught a whole generation to sneer at achievement in public life, although Amiel also dismissively (and with some apparent inconsistency) suggests that this amounts more than anything else to a confirmation of a pre-existing climate of opinion, and that the programme is not likely to change people's ideas significantly. The former Conservative prime minister Edward Heath, who affects inability to recall the programme's title, describes it in similar terms as a symptom of envy felt by irresponsible mediocrities for those who have achieved fame or success.

Spitting Image and the political process

In the course of discussion (and video editing), the question whether *Spitting Image* is a good thing or a bad one gets inextricably entangled with another – in principle, entirely separate – question as to its real effects on the political process in general and on the fortunes of the Liberal–Social Democrat Alliance at the 1987 general election in particular. Thus Hattersley argues that the programme did have an effect, and indeed a negative one, on the Alliance because it highlighted what was already a point of vulnerability, namely its joint leadership by the leaders of its two constituent parties, David Owen and David Steel. Steel himself, apparently anxious not to seem querulous at the damage he and his party have supposedly been done, describes *Spitting Image* as being 'very funny'. In Steel's case as in Hattersley's, positive evaluation of the programme goes with a belief that its constant harping on the joint leadership, and its portrayal of Owen as being dominant in the partnership, did indeed damage the Alliance's fortunes. Conversely, both Day and Heath dissent from the view that *Spitting Image* did the Alliance any significant damage, preferring to see its portrayal as a more or less straightforward and accurate reflection of prior realities.

To summarize: it is on grounds of *Spitting Image*'s alleged but controversial political influence and cultural lineage that Bragg is able to describe it as 'an institution of British TV', to initiate a debate on this subject with leading public and establishment figures, and to transmit this debate on one of the UK's best-known cultural review TV programmes. But the terms of that debate as we have summarized it are misplaced, at least in the sense that they do not engage with some of the most obvious, and interesting, features of *Spitting Image*. Bragg's own programme is in our view more interesting when the discussion moves away from the question of *Spitting Image*'s influence on voting behaviour and treatment of specific issues, and instead focuses on the part the programme plays in the reduction of politics to a matter of personalities.

At one point, for example, a former *Spitting Image* producer claims that the programme is instrumental in acquainting viewers with politicians whose identities are not otherwise impressed upon them by the news and current affairs media. For instance, he suggests that government ministers otherwise eclipsed by Margaret Thatcher in fact first became widely known in the form of their *Spitting Image* puppets. Roy Hattersley endorses this view, reporting that children in schools he has visited ask him about his *Spitting Image* puppet before they ask him about political issues. These remarks add an elementary concept of mediation to the view of the relationship between *Spitting Image* and politics evident in the discussion of the 1987 election. Some such concept would be a necessary part of any plausible ascription of real political effects to the programme, particularly given that *Spitting Image* treated politicians of all persuasions in very much the same way. Such a concept would, however, also be consistent with a number of the descriptions of *Spitting Image* previously quoted from the *South Bank Show* programme which dismiss it as trivial and vulgar entertainment. It is therefore the key to an economical but effective understanding of the programme in itself, and an illustration of the way televisual meanings generally are produced and exchanged.

The experience Hattersley reports was probably only possible because *Spitting Image* foregrounded his personality and idiosyncratic manner of speaking at the expense of the policies he espoused. Similarly, the image of a squeaky-voiced puppet of David Steel, popping out of David Owen's pocket or sitting precariously poised on the edge of a settee, framed in memorable televisual imagery a number of observations that had already been well established in other ways – that Steel was 'in Owen's pocket' and that his position was a vulnerable one. Other scenes often showed Steel looking up with a sycophantic smile at a dominant and frowning Owen (figure 1). By doing this, however, they added to such views of the Alliance leadership a significant element of the ludicrous and the pathetic, the latter term being used here in its strong sense to mean that pathos is created. The *South Bank Show*'s emphasis on discussing *Spitting Image*'s direct political effect without reference to

1 *Spitting Image*: the two Davids

the mediation of its political content through this kind of intrinsically televisual meaning ignores the crucial role which television itself played in the programme, and thus misses what seems to us to be the key element in the programme's organization, its continuing success with viewers, and its possible effect in shaping viewers' perceptions of the personalities of public life.

Appropriation of *Spitting Image* in the *South Bank Show*

We conclude our discussion of the *South Bank Show* programme by recapitulating what we consider to be the three major points emerging from it.

In the first place, *Spitting Image* is assimilated to a pre-televisual tradition of political satire, although this suggestion is not based on any serious textual or intertextual analysis of the programme or of the tradition. Whatever else this may mean, a high degree of cultural legitimacy is certainly attributed to *Spitting Image* by those participants in the programme who support such views (Bragg, Hattersley), and to a lesser extent by the other well-known figures who appear on the programme to express a strong positive appreciation of *Spitting Image* (Steel). Yet even by the standards of their own social, cultural and political milieu, these views of *Spitting Image* are controversial: witness the remarks made by Amiel, Day and Heath.

Secondly, the absence of any textual or intertextual analysis of the programme means that the precise causes of its allegedly substantial real effects on the electoral process remain unspecified (and this remains the case whether or not it actually had any such effects). In any case, no empirical data are given concerning *Spitting Image*'s audience and its reception of the programme, and this means that the effects postulated are more a matter of supposition than of evidence and argument.

Thirdly, we feel bound to underline the fact that all this happens on the *South Bank Show*, where culture is implicitly defined in honorific terms. During the 1980s and 1990s the increasing complexity and fluidity of the cultural and economic structure of society at large (which obviously also means that of the television audience) was widely noted (in this book, see also Chapters 2 and 7). Nonetheless, Bragg's references to the satirical draughtsmen of the eighteenth and nineteenth centuries implies a conception of culture and, in particular, of cultural tradition that is quite clearly class-specific, in the sense of being a mark of social distinction (Bourdieu 1984). In other words, the terms of Bragg's argument lift *Spitting Image* out of the circuit of communication and the context of popular culture in relation to which it would have to be studied if the questions raised in the first two paragraphs of this concluding summary were to be posed in any very consequential way.

Alternative analysis of *Spitting Image*

We now set out our own provisional account of what *Spitting Image* was and how it worked. This argument falls into three parts.

1. That *Spitting Image* homogenized a range of otherwise generally distinct TV genres, assimilating them to an all-embracing category of fictionality.

2. That it worked even on news and current affairs television in this way, so that they were brought within the range of the programme's characteristic form of fictional light entertainment; this laid emphasis on the ways in which its subject matter – including that borrowed from current affairs broadcasting – was mediated, rather than on the subject matter itself.

3. That by the early 1990s, although this was not necessarily the case earlier on, *Spitting Image* could most accurately have been described by the phrase 'TV pastiche'; indeed, some episodes are structured in a way that seems to parody not only particular programmes and genres, but a whole evening's schedule.

TV genre recycled

To have been able to decode every reference *Spitting Image* made, you would have had to spend a very great deal of time watching TV. Indeed, the pleasure to be had from watching *Spitting Image* was clearly a matter of recognizing cross-references to other domains of everyday knowledge, including those of popular culture and television. In the literature on the formats of popular culture and their audiences (whether this relates to game and quiz shows with their intertextual references, to soap operas, to advertising or to whatever other comparable genre), the positive evaluation of these formats hinges precisely on the active viewing in which audiences engage as their everyday knowledge and interests are aroused. This kind of active response is frequently evoked by writers concerned to question the dismissal of such formats as low-quality mass culture (see Fiske 1978; and, in this volume, Chapters 6 and 7). Certainly by the 1990s *Spitting Image* did not regularly privilege political subject matter, and therefore could not be appropriately classified as political satire, whatever its effects on voting behaviour. The following examples illustrate the blending together of a range of TV genres within which fictional, political and other well-known media-related figures come to cohabit in extraordinary promiscuity.

Mastermind revisited

The episode of *Spitting Image* broadcast on 9 December 1991 included a sketch featuring the then president of the United States of America, George Bush, appearing in the format of the BBC quiz show *Mastermind*, hosted by Magnus Magnusson. Contestants on this programme answered questions on a specialist subject of their own choice as well as on a range of general knowledge topics. Bush's specialist subject was democracy, with particular reference to Kuwait (a country which had at the beginning of the year been liberated by United States forces based in neighbouring Saudi Arabia from occupation by the Iraqi army commanded by dictator Saddam Hussein). The first four lines of dialogue and the penultimate one replicate Magnusson's formal, somewhat ritualistic, manner, which was a hallmark of the BBC programme:

MM Your name?

GB George Bush.

MM And your specialist subject?

GB Democracy!

MM Which country allows only seven per cent of its population to vote?

GB Iraq!

MM No, Kuwait!

MM Which country was condemned by Amnesty International in November of this year for the systematic torture of a minority population?

GB Iraq!

MM No, Saudi Arabia!

MM Which country's invasion of an independent state was condemned by the UN General Assembly resolution no. 44/240?

GB Iraq!

MM No, America's invasion of Panama!

MM Ten other countries have been invaded in the last two decades. Why were no American troops sent to assist?

GB Ehm, pass!

MM President Bush, you scored no points. You passed on only one, why were no American troops sent to assist the ten other countries, and the answer is because they don't produce lots of cheap oil!

GB Damn, I knew that one!

Here, the combination of the quiz-show format with political subject matter might seem to support the thesis that *Spitting Image* is political satire, since Bush repeatedly suggests Iraq is the country violating civil rights and condemned by Amnesty International for torturing members of a minority population. In displaying his profound ignorance of his chosen 'specialist' subject, democracy, Bush's wrong answers satirically stress the point that other countries than Iraq have dubious civil rights records, and that the United States' own foreign policy is more marked by expediency than by any more idealistic motivation. However, the force of the sketch depends on Bush's appearing in an inappropriate generic format at least as much as on the political point being made, which is, in any case, exceptionally biting for this phase of *Spitting Image*'s history.

Sextalk and *Question Time* revisited

The episode of *Spitting Image* broadcast on 25 November 1991 provides a rather more typical example of a politician's appearing in an inappropriate context. Roy Hattersley's puppet is inserted into the format of the Channel 4 chat show *Sextalk*, but the lines it speaks convey quite clearly a mistaken belief that he is appearing on the political discussion programme *Question Time*. Even though the sketch features other well-known figures from the realms of politics (David Owen and the notoriously aggressive Northern Ireland Protestant leader, the Reverend Ian Paisley, who appears as a heckler) but also entertainment (the rock singer Rod Stewart and the television comedians Ben Elton and Stephen Fry), this mistake continues to the end and is never resolved. Hattersley's disorientation is a matter of knockabout farce rather than of political satire; the focus is on a personality rather than on anything that has a bearing on questions of policy.

Another important figure who appears in the same *Sextalk* sketch is Prince Edward, presumably selected for inclusion because he had relatively recently left the Royal Marines for a show-business career amid accusations of effeminacy from the popular press. However, several members of the royal family were among *Spitting Image*'s most commonly featured characters, and appear with some frequency in a range of more or less unexpected situations. For instance, the episode of 11 November 199 features the whole family, dressed for the occasion, in a rap-music video, with grotesquely sycophantic commentary by Sir Alistair Burnett, the Independent Television News journalist famous also for his royal interviews. The same episode also features the Prince and Princess of Wales enacting a domestic drama recalling format, styles and themes of soap opera. Indeed, the regular appearance of the Windsors as a family with domestic problems and shown in domestic settings is very typical of the transgeneric fictionalizing pastiche we have suggested is characteristic of *Spitting Image*.

The royal family: soap revisited

The creation of a glamorous ideal family comprising the monarch's more or less immediate relatives by blood and marriage has only taken place during the last 150 years, since Queen Victoria's reign. Gradually, but always as a matter of deliberate policy involving royalty, government and media, the royal family has been fabricated and its family life staged as a focus of identification for the common people, and thus of national and social cohesion. This image is invoked time and time again by *Spitting Image*, but always returned – parodically – to the ordinary domestic scene. Whether it is a matter of tension caused within a marriage by the absence of sexual relations (Di and Charles, the Prince and Princess of Wales, in the sketch just mentioned), or of parental absenteeism (as suggested in lines sung in the music-video sketch by Andrew and Fergie, the Duke and Duchess of York), the relationships and tensions shown are familiar everyday ones. This is echoed by the way the puppets are dressed. Queen Elizabeth II, for example, wears her famous headscarf, but instead of signalling a visit to her stables or a family stroll on one of the royal estates, as it would elsewhere than in *Spitting Image*, she wears it to cover a set of curlers. This kind of image is more familiar from programmes such as *Coronation Street* or *Eastenders* than from conventional media coverage of the royal family. The royal crown, slipped in between the curlers and the scarf, looks like cheap jewellery from a market stall (figure 2).

This slippage from the royal domain to the most ordinary domestic life is a continuous theme in *Spitting Image*, and contrasts in its mild and affectionate irony with the harsh sensationalist treatment of certain members of the royal family in the popular press. It is therefore no surprise that the esteem in which the royal family is held is not negatively affected by their appearance as puppets on *Spitting Image*. A paper by Wober from the ITC even suggests that 'there was actually a positive relationship between the amount of viewing *Spitting Image* received, and esteem for senior royal figures' (Wober 1992: 1). The anecdotal evidence of a report published in the *Guardian* on 24 January 1997 also suggests an increase in Yasser Arafat's popularity in Israel after he began to be depicted on *Hartzufim*.

2 *Spitting Image*: the Queen

Leaking genres

Sometimes the kind of leakage between genres that we have been discussing with reference to *Spitting Image*'s handling of the royal family itself becomes the subject of the programme and an occasion of humour. One instance of this is the case of a potato that migrates from one TV genre to another with almost bewildering rapidity. After escaping from the disintegrating USSR, where economic mismanagement and food shortages had placed it in danger of being eaten, it is engaged in conversation – in his own home, during a tiff with his wife – by the Prince of Wales (whose more notorious eccentricities at the time included a habit of conversing with vegetables). In the same programme the same dissident and refugee potato will show up at a meeting of the Labour shadow cabinet and be subjected to torture by Saddam Hussein.

This leakage between TV genres is not original to *Spitting Image*: it is a typical feature of TV advertising, music videos and contemporary television generally. For instance, the distinctive face-to-face dialogue format of the comedy programme *Smith and Jones* passed over into a Nationwide Anglia Building Society TV commercial: it is a particularly pertinent example because it was then taken up by

Spitting Image in the episode of 9 December 1991, in a sketch where two seal-puppets, filmed in the same configuration and speaking in recognizable Smith-and-Jones voices, reflect on the hazards of marine life in the seal-culling season.

The range of television genres recycled on *Spitting Image* (and frequently signalled by the appearance of puppets representing their distinctive personnel among other means) is all but exhaustive, including virtually every conceivable format. Weather forecasts feature Ian McCaskill, notorious for the eccentricity both of his presentation and of much of his material, as well as for the sheer length of time he has maintained this act. Natural science documentaries (for example, a sketch on the urban fox on 25 November 1992) offered an occasion to exhibit prominently a puppet of the best known of natural-science programme makers, David Attenborough. But there are also more purely generic parodies of religious broadcasting and of a range of popular films and TV serials. Some of these were shown in separate episodes week by week, including in the early 1990s a regular dose of *Teenage Mutant Ninja Turds*, parodying the *Teenage Mutant Ninja Turtles* film/television series/printed comic strip/merchandising phenomenon of the time.

Television genre as pastiche

In the light of this general description of *Spitting Image* in the early 1990s, we can now return to the question of political satire. In the context of *Spitting Image*'s general tendency to TV pastiche, news and current affairs formats are assimilated to light entertainment. What happens is not so much that events, persons or processes in the world are satirized but rather, much more commonly, that the TV formats of their representation are parodied.

News as seen on TV

On 18 November 1991 a sketch featured the sometime transport minister Cecil Parkinson trying to schedule a disaster in the Channel Tunnel and thereby attract media coverage. What is brought into focus here is the way newsworthy events, including political ones but not only them, are orchestrated in order to fit into broadcasting schedules in such a way that maximum coverage is guaranteed, and, sometimes, that maximum advantage can be extracted from this. In the *Spitting Image* sketch, Parkinson's carefully planned appearance at the scene of the disaster, to see for himself, which is to be followed by a visit to the injured in hospital, is disrupted by an unforeseen explosion. If the effect is satirical, it does not bear on political issues current at the time but on the way news events in general tend to take place in a form partly predetermined by patterns of television coverage and consumption. However, it is precisely this tendency to thematize the forms and processes of communication that we wish to highlight by opting to characterize *Spitting Image* as pastiche or parody rather than as satire, which we would take to involve a quite different kind of emphasis, on issues and personalities whose significance (and suitability as targets for satire) would normally be considered to consist in something more (and perhaps more serious from a political or moral point of view) than simple involvement in even a highly visible public spectacle such as television.

News presenters as seen on TV

This shift away from treatment of substantive topics in politics and current affairs often leads to emphasis being placed on the forms and personalities of news mediation. The episode of 11 November 1992 includes a sketch in which the puppet representing Michael Heseltine physically attempts to displace Jeremy Paxman, then a regular presenter of *Newsnight*, the BBC's most serious weekday news programme, from his chair in front of the camera. Heseltine himself had recently been the first to challenge the then prime minister, Margaret Thatcher, for the leadership of the Conservative Party (figure 3), but in this sketch the pursuit of media exposure and control of media coverage is accorded priority over that of high office. Not only are news and current affairs broadcasters such as Paxman (and, on other occasions, Trevor MacDonald of Independent Television News) given the same weight and coverage in *Spitting Image* as the politicians on whose doings it is elsewhere their *raison d'être* to report and comment, they are also treated more sympathetically. The specific episode just mentioned culminates in another sketch where Heseltine crosses the border into madness as he outlines his plans to replace neither Thatcher nor Paxman, but rather God. Taken as a whole, the episode's parody of an evening's

3 *Spitting Image*: Michael and Maggie

TV schedule leads from this disrupted edition of *Newsnight* to a weather report featuring Ian McCaskill, who is treated in humorous terms quite lacking the acidic edge of the way Heseltine is presented.

Closed-circuit intertexuality: *Spitting Image* on *Spitting Image*

The predominant tendency to media pastiche illustrated by these examples is taken to its logical conclusion in a series-within-the-series entitled 'Some of Our Puppets Are Missing' and focusing on the production of *Spitting Image* itself. Here, a group of puppets including both David Steel and Mr Spock from the science-fiction serial *Star Trek* escape into the real world where they are seen mingling with natural human figures rather than latex puppets. Their astonishment at finding themselves among carbon-based life forms without a trace of rubber, which do not even, as Mr Spock remarks, 'appear to have hands stuck up their bottoms', underlines *Spitting Image*'s primary, parodic, focus on television itself. David Steel's delight that he will no longer be 'made to look stupid' clearly illustrates *Spitting Image*'s relationship to politics, which is one of entertainment, parody and simplification along personalized lines. *Spitting Image*'s entertainment value surely derived from the way it pointed up and made play with the things we already half-knew about television itself, and about the ways in which, perhaps increasingly, television programmes are conceived and watched.

We have argued in this chapter that the satirical stance of *Spitting Image*, while clearly feeding on and off personalities from the public sphere, is better understood if approached from the vantage point of popular culture and entertainment. Popular culture's appetite for generic hybridity (see also Chapter 4 in this volume) and the recycling of its own themes and forms in a continuous chain of re-representations informs all the *Spitting Image* sketches we have discussed here. It is to be assumed that the pleasure which viewers experienced in watching them owed at least as much, if not more, to their intertextual recognition of 'life as seen on TV' as to any more strenuous satirical commentary on political processes.

References

Bourdieu, P. (1984), *Distinction: A Social Critique of the Judgement of Taste*, London: Routledge.

Fairclough, N. (1995), *Media Discourse*, London: Arnold.

Fiske, J. (1978), *Reading Television*, London: Methuen.

Masterman, L. (1994), *Teaching the Media*, London: Routledge.

Wagg, S. (1992), 'You've never had it so silly. The politics of British satirical comedy from *Beyond the Fringe To Spitting Image*', in D. Strinati and S. Wagg (eds), *Come on Down? Popular Media Culture in Post-War Britain*, London: Routledge, 254–84.

Wober, J. (1992), 'TV satire and the monarchy', *Independent TV Research Department*, February, 1–18.

Viewers' worlds: image, music, text and the *Rock 'n' Roll Years*[1]

ULRIKE H. MEINHOF AND THEO VAN LEEUWEN

Media discourse analysis has been centrally influenced by the French semiologist Roland Barthes, in particular by his early study *Mythologies* ([1957] 1973) and the collection of essays *Image – Music – Text* from 1977, which includes the essay 'The rhetoric of the image'. In the latter, Barthes discusses the question of how the linguistic and the iconic components of a text contribute to its meaning. Barthes sees images as essentially polysemous, open to many readings or interpretations. Language can fix the fluid character of the image (or other more polysemic modes such as music) by narrowing the meaning down to a selection of possible readings. Barthes calls this anchorage – a function he finds typically fulfilled by captions to press photographs or ads. Less frequently, language can also enter a complementary relationship with the image, typically seen in some cartoons or comic strips, where the unity of the message is realized at the higher level of the narrative. This relation he describes as relay. Barthes' analysis, accompanied by many examples from advertising and film stills, became centrally important in the study of media texts with strong visual (for example, billboard adverts) or audiovisual elements (for example, most of what we see and hear on television or the Internet).

Following on from Barthes, other writers, ourselves included, have argued that this priorization on the verbal over the visual and other modes does not fully allow for the fact that these modes, though interdependent with the verbal, are nevertheless independently structured (see, for example, Meinhof 1994, Kress and van Leeuwen 1996). Multimodality in this perspective is conceived as the interaction of different modes, each contributing different elements of meaning, which may or may not support one another.

It is, for example, perfectly feasible that the relationship between different modes is conflictual rather than supportive or complementary. As Kress shows in this volume, making meaning from texts is a continuous process of semiosis which readers/viewers achieve through simultaneously engaging with different textual modes, all of which interact with one another. Such a reading then shifts the source of meaning away from textual codes on to the interaction with these potentially conflicting codes by viewers.

This emphasis on the viewer has important consequences for how intertextuality is conceived. Rather than seeing texts as carriers of intertextual references to other textual forms which may be coded in one of several textual modes, intertextual readings now comprise the many different social and cultural reference points which viewers use in the process of making meanings. This does not deny the text any of its multimodal complexity. But an analysis of how meanings are made by readers/viewers must now also incorporate the intertextual reference points which they bring to bear in their engagement with the text. Multimodal readings are thus by definition multiple and open to divergence, according to the knowledge, attitudes and beliefs of viewers.

Yet such readings are not entirely unique or idiosyncratic either, but are made in response to texts which are themselves conceivable in larger units than just singular instances. These higher-level units – or genres – not only organize texts into patterns by generalizing areas of likely meanings, they also influence the way viewers anticipate, take note of and judge what they see: a TV commercial will arouse different expectations and assessments than a music video or a news text (Meinhof 1993 and 1998). There is thus a dynamic interplay between genres, texts and viewers. Viewers' expectations will be formed about a type of text in response to generic principles, rather than just a single textual instance. The multimodal textual instance, on the other hand, may draw on much more than what is generically predictable. Modern media, in particular, are full of hybrid forms which do not comply with any obvious generic model.

Rock 'n' Roll Years

The television series *Rock 'n' Roll Years* provides us with an excellent example of just such a hybrid. As a series it is difficult to place in generic terms. A combination of newsreel documentation and musical extracts from a series of thirty years in as many thirty-minute programmes, *Rock 'n' Roll Years* appears to be almost a genre in its own right. This does not mean that it is unique in every respect. It combines methods familiar from the compilation documentary with the techniques of modern advertising, popular music videos and other genres of highly allusive, polyphonic text. It blends images and music into a single unit of audiovisual text, with complex interconnections between the visual and the aural channel. And it is sprinkled with citations, like many contemporary pop videos – Freddy Mercury and Queen's pop video for their song 'Radio ga ga', for instance, parodies scenes from Fritz Lang's celebrated expressionist film *Metropolis*. In a video produced by German film maker Wim Wenders for the song 'Stay' by the Irish rock band U2, the lead singer Bono perches on top of the Berlin Statue of Liberty, just as the angel did in Wenders' feature film *Der Himmel über Berlin* (Wings of Desire). And Bono, like the angel in the film, also swoops down to assist ordinary humans, in this case by playing and singing for an anonymous rock band. Everyone will know dozens of similar examples from film and television. There is thus some similarity in the organization of these audiovisual texts and in the 'postmodern' viewing habits which are clearly presupposed both for viewers of *Rock 'n' Roll Years* and those of music videos and other related genres. Viewers must tolerate and enjoy allusions, citations, quick episodic flashes, a kaleidoscope of impressions, rather than depend on realistic, consistent or transparent narratives.

Structure of the programme

In order to analyse the series in detail, we will select one of its programmes, the one that deals with the year 1968. To explain why we chose 1968, we need to refer back to the seminal text by Roland Barthes mentioned in the opening paragraph, his *Mythologies*. Barthes famously explained how the denotative element of a sign, that which it literally depicts, is complemented by its connotative quality, the associative meanings which it inspires. He also shows how connotations can become naturalized to such an extent that they take over and replace any appeal to an external referent, such as a historical moment. Myth, Barthes writes, 'transforms history into nature' (Barthes 1973: 129); it is 'depoliticized speech' (142). The year

1968 has achieved mythical status in that it is often quoted as representative of the entire decade of the 1960s, arousing connotations of energy and youthfulness, revolt against tradition. By concentrating on its treatment of the year 1968, it will be interesting to see whether *Rock 'n' Roll Years* shares or subverts the mythology of the 1960s and how viewers responded to the programme's appeal.

In the series each year is given an independent thirty-minute treatment, so the programme about 1968 is the ninth covering the decade. All events and soundtracks relate strictly to that year, with forty-two news stories and twenty-three songs from the same year selected and edited. Apart from newsreels about the Paris student uprising, selected news stories include, for example, extracts about the reporting of world events such as the political liberalization in Czechoslovakia under Dubček, to so-called 'Prague Spring', and later that year its brutal suppression by the invasion of the Soviet Army; the famous 'promised land' speech by the black American civil rights leader Martin Luther King, as well as his tragic assassination and funeral, and the assassination of US senator Robert Kennedy, brother of the former US president John F. Kennedy, as he was himself campaigning for presidential election. They include news clips about a famine in the African state of Biafra, which killed thousands of people, as well as an inflammatory speech against the immigration policy of the British government by right-wing politician Enoch Powell. But they also comprise 'soft news', such as a clip about the launching of space-ship *Apollo*, sports events, extracts from rock concerts such as the last concert by British rock group the Cream, an interview with John Lennon from the Beatles, clips about disc jockeys, media commentators, etc. The presentation of the news clips is kaleidoscopic: items which in an ordinary news broadcast would be strictly ordered by their social or political significance appear side by side. For example, a sports item such as a cricket player breaking the world record appears next to the assassination of Robert Kennedy, followed by the US pediatrician-writer Dr Spock being sent to prison for supporting draft-dodging during the time of the Vietnam War. In this mixture of anecdotal and heavy politics the programme offers a typical postmodern spectrum where events are rendered equivalent, without any hierarchy or priorization. (For a theoretical debate on these issues in postmodernism, see for example Jameson 1984 and 1991, Eco 1986, Bandrillard 1988, especially Chapter 8.)

With two or three noticeable exceptions, such as the assassination of Robert Kennedy, where part of the original soundtrack is kept, most news stories are shown as film footage only, with added-on captions identifying the events. Replacing the original news soundtracks are twenty-three songs selected from the popular music released during the same year. The news items and songs are incomplete extracts of varying length and with different boundaries. Several news flashes may have the same song accompanying them, or two or three different soundtracks may accompany the same news event. Selection and editing together of news and music is highly specific in each instance, with the news commenting on the music or the music commenting on the news event in different but clearly marked ways. In this combination of news footage and popular-music sound, each genre loses its original function: news extracts no longer report current affairs, song extracts are no longer the top hits of the moment. Together they take on an altogether different function, interpreting a particular year in the recent past, but not by the usual documentary methods, nor even by documentary montage, but by symbolic representation. *Rock 'n' Roll Years* is thus neither a documentary about the events of a particular year, nor simply a music programme, but a metadocumentary, where the items, as combined, provide a symptomatic reading of each year at a time through an accumulation of allusions and references, and through connotation rather than through denotation. This will become clear if we look at some extracts in more detail.

The extract below forms the beginning of the 1968 programme. It illustrates most of the types of interaction between music and newsreel extracts in *Rock 'n' Roll Years*. Its opening song, 'Quinn the Eskimo', written by Bob Dylan, was made famous in 1968 in the version as performed here, by the Manfred Mann band. The music is a rousing hymn in praise of drugs (sugar). It speaks the musical language of the rousing anthem (cf. Marothy 1974: 56ff.), the song that energetically rallies people together for common action, just as we find it, for instance, in Christmas carols like 'Oh come, all ye faithful'. It is set in a major key, with a 4/4 marching tempo and dotted rhythms in the melody (DAA-de-DAA-de-DAA). The song opens with a kind of pied-piper introduction, played on the flute. The musical message is the same as the message of the lyrics: come to me, come and join! On the lines 'But when Quinn the Eskimo gets here, everybody's gonna jump for joy', the march rhythm stops and holds its breath, as it were, and a heavenly choir of soft wordless female voices accompanies. Then, on 'Come all within', the rhythm starts again:[2]

1	CS flautist	*'Pied piper' flute intro*
2	MS Manfred Mann, from low angle. Camera slowly zooms in to VCS.	'Everybody's building Ships and boats Some are building monuments Others jotting down notes Everybody's in despair Every girl and boy'
3	MS three members of the band	'But when Quinn the Eskimo gets here Everybody's gonna jump for joy'
4	CS keyboard player	'Come all without'
5	CS drummer	'Come all within'
6	CS guitarist	'You won't see nothing like the mighty Quinn'
7	CS flautist	*'Pied piper' flute intro*
8	CS Mann, in profile. From time to time he turns to face the camera.	'I like to go just like the rest I like my sugar sweet But jumping queues and making haste Just ain't my cup of meat Everyone's beneath the trees Feeding pigeons on a limb'
9	*Red-edged wipe to* MS Dubček seated behind table in conference hall, with people behind him applauding	'When Quinn the Eskimo gets here All the pigeons gonna run'
	Subtitle: Alexander Dubček is elected First Secretary	
10	LS conference hall, full of people	'... to him'
11	MCS Dubček shouting at audience, his hands around his mouth, then waves at them	'Come all without Come all within'
	Subtitle: He begins a process of liberalisation	
12	MCS crowd in streets, waving flags as they move past dignitaries on a balcony	'You won't ...'
13	MS man carried by crowd, playing guitar and then raising the guitar above his head in a triumphant gesture	'... see nothing like the ...'

14 MS another man carried by crowd. Camera tilts up to the American flag which he is carrying	'... mighty Quinn'
15 High angle of people waving flags	'Come all without'
Subtitle: The Czech people celebrate their new freedom	
16 CS man in crowd, applauding	'Come all within'
17 CS crowd, camera panning to stop on CS woman who looks up at something, smiling	'You won't see nothing like the mighty ...'
18 High angle of people waving flags. *Freeze frame as we hear a gunshot*	'... Quinn ...'
19 Red-edged zig-zag wipe to LS American Embassy in Vietnam. Helmeted US soldiers seek cover behind low wall.	*Moody blues music starts on gunshot*
Subtitle: The Vietcong launches widespread attacks in South Vietnam	

Like many of the key sequences of the programme, this segment begins with sync footage of a rock 'n' roll band. But after a while the images of singer(s) and players make place for newsreel footage of the Prague Spring of 1968. This footage now (re)interprets the song. It provides us with a specific reference for Quinn the Eskimo, an enigmatic figure except for those who recognize the in-group reference to the dope dealer. How specific this reinterpretation is depends on how much we already know about the events, since the information provided in the subtitles is minimal. At the same time the song also (re)interprets the images: Dubček becomes Quinn the Eskimo, the dope dealer, and the pied piper of the intro. He becomes associated with other references as well. As the words 'the mighty Quinn' are repeated over and over, they coincide, not only with our first view of Dubček, but also with shots of a rock guitar (shot 13) and an American flag (shot 14), both of them standing out in the stream of images through movements of the people in the shot or of the camera. And as the words 'Come all ...' are repeated over and over, we see shots of enthusiastic crowds waving and applauding – for the merged messages of Manfred Mann and Alexander Dubček. In all this the images do not fully explain the lyrics, nor the lyrics the images. Rather, the images link a specific event and a specific person to the more allusive and elusive events and people of the lyrics (elusive, that is, for those who do not possess the dope-culture references).

At the same time the lyrics and music provide connotative generalization, a broader interpretation and an emotive feel for the news event, and they also facilitate an association of the various images that receive their rhythmic accents from the key words of the lyrics (van Leeuwen 1985). A rhythm responded to, allusive words repeated over and over, images of Dubcêk, a guitar, an American flag, a face in the crowd – from such disparate elements an overall feel for the mood of the beginning of 1968 emerges from the start of the programme.

Another example. In the images we see, in big sweaty close-ups, Mick Jagger and the other Rolling Stones performing the song 'Jumpin' Jack Flash'. The music is dominated by an energetic back-beat and by Jagger's hard, tense, raw and rasping voice:

I was born in a crossfire hurricane
And I howled at my ma in the driving rain
But it's all right now
In fact it's a gas
But it's all right
I'm Jumpin' Jack Flash
It's a gas, gas, gas

I was raised by a toothless bearded hag
I was schooled with a strap across my bag
But it's all right now
In fact it's a gas
But it's all right
I'm Jumpin' Jack Flash
It's a gas, gas, gas.

The programme cuts to newsreel images of Paris, May 1968, at the beginning of an instrumental break. Imagine the following images rhythmicized by driving guitar riffs, the raw energy of a loud drumming, and occasional vocalizations such as 'Yeah!', 'Oooh', etc.

1 MLS helmeted policeman throwing something at a throng of protesters on a Paris boulevard, the handheld camera panning along with whatever he is throwing	*Jumpin' Jack Flash: instrumental break* 'Yeah … whooah …'

Subtitle: PARIS
    Students and workers unite in
    violent clashes with the police

2   MLS policeman hitting a man with his
    baton

3   MLS ambulance, camera panning with it

    Subtitle: Students have denounced the
      established university system …

4   MLS smoke-filled street, with policeman   'Whooah!'
    running through the smoke

5   MCS group of police, camera following
    them from behind as they charge into
    protesters

6   MLS police van being rocked

    Subtitle: … as a product of bourgeois
      society.

7   MLS fire on the streets, a car turning
    back to avoid it

8   Newspaper headline: 'I won't allow
    anarchy, says de Gaulle.'

9   LS crowd in streets, joining hands.   'Watch it!'

    Subtitle: France is brought to a standstill
      by a general strike

10 MLS two policemen in front of banner
    ('The bank is closed')

    Subtitle: Prime Minister Pompidou claims   *3rd stanza starts:*
      there has been an attempt …   'I was drowned …'

11 Banner in red paint: unlimited strike   'I was washed up'

12 LS shopping street with garbage piling up   'Left for …'

13 LS church with piles of garbage in front of it   '… dead'

    Subtitle: … to start a civil war.

14 CS BBC interviewer   *music fades out*
                        (sync) 'Just how far is France from
    Subtitle: Michael Blekey   civil war at the moment'

15 CS Cohn-Bendit   'Oh, very far because to have a
                        a civil war you need two parties in
    Subtitle: Daniel Cohn-Bendit, student leader   the population and here you haven't.
                        You have on one side the police
                        and on the other side the population.
                        So you don't have a civil war.'

16	CS BBC interviewer	'And how do you hope it will all end eventually?'
17	CS Cohn-Bendit	'I can now see that it can end in the best way, with a new government'
18	LS crowd on Paris boulevard	'But I think that the people have learnt ...'
19	CS Cohn-Bendit	'... that they can change something if they go into the streets or the factory.'

On its own, especially without any clear reference to May 1968, and without the music, the newsreel presents images of destruction and upheaval. Cars are burning, violence is erupting in the street between protesters and police. But the music re-signifies these images with an optimistic and energetic feeling, and the lyrics link the political rebellion against the system with the personal and emotive rebellion against the older generation – here without the close ties between specific words and specific images which we saw in the other excerpt. What matters most here is injecting these events with a particular recognizable emotion, with a sense of excitement and energy.

What emerges is an interpretation of 1968 which collapses the heterogeneity and polyphony of the different images and texts into a rather nostalgic 'Do you remember?' The statements of Cohn-Bendit come at the end of the section, and are therefore already anchored in the emotive drive and raw energy of the music, in the way that the images of reality we see in news and current affairs items are already anchored by the anchor person's or newsreader's introduction.

Overall, then, it is the music which is thematic, the music which leads each major segment. The programme is in the first place a compilation of 1968 rock 'n' roll numbers. But it is also a programme about a particular year, and that year is characterized by its key world events, as defined by the media. The two elements then merge and intertwine, and the music interprets the events, and provides them with emotive colour, in a process of connotative generalization.

Some of the links between words and images, however, do not contribute to this connotative and interpretive process, and merely serve to provide a shallow and gratuitous link between a song and an event. When Alan Price, in the song 'Don't stop the carnival', gets to the line 'But this is England on a winter's afternoon', for example, we cut to shots of Jean Claude Killy winning three gold medals for skiing in the 1968 Winter Olympics. When the Bonzo Dog Band plays 'I'm an urban space man' we cut to the launch of spaceship *Apollo 8*. Here the words of the song merely provide an excuse for introducing the next newsreel clip, rather than providing interpretation or emotive resonance.

Word–picture relations may also be ironic. As we see Asians entering England from Nairobi, we hear Cilla Black sing 'Step inside love', a soft bossa-nova beat behind her. Anyone wishing to read this as a well-meaning commentary on how England receives its Commonwealth population with open arms is quickly disabused of that notion by the following extract. Here the lines 'What's the ugliest part of your body ... I think it's your mind' from a song by Frank Zappa and the Mothers of Invention becomes a bitterly sarcastic comment on Enoch Powell's speech against immigration policy. Equally ironic, though more poignantly expressed, is the connection between Louis Armstrong's 'It's a wonderful world', which follows Martin Luther King's 'promised land' speech, accompanying news footage of his funeral, which in turn anticipates Robert Kennedy's assassination later that year by prominently showing him amongst the mourners.

Encoding and decoding language and image

The extracts quoted show that *Rock 'n' Roll Years* offers a complex interaction between channels, more so than many other TV genres. In news items, for example, texts and pictures clash in ways which require the viewer to infer across channels to form single representations of the reported events. Inferences are highly responsive to the viewer's world knowledge, their willingness and ability to activate different knowledge structures such as schemata (see for example van Dijk and Kintsch 1983). But news broadcasts within a particular society for particular social groups are clearly targeted at a presupposed audience with sets of assumed knowledges. A report about a home event or a striking international story will thus have a very different organization from a report about an event where little knowledge can be assumed. The information content and the relationship between the two channels is thus more tightly controlled to direct viewers to a particular preferred reading of the news item, where a particular transfer of information is to happen, which, of course, may or may not take place. The difference between this kind of assumed interaction between encoding and decoding in news items and the kind of interaction taking place in *Rock 'n' Roll Years* could not be greater. The news requires a certain denotative closure, at least in principle. If this does not occur, viewers will simply not process what is the essential information content of the item. In *Rock 'n' Roll Years* and other similar genres such denotative closure is less important. Not all references and allusions need to be grasped by every viewer, and not every word of the lyrics needs to be heard. On the other hand, there may be greater connotative closure – it is essential that the May 1968 revolt of Paris be linked to the music of the Rolling Stones. All viewers will recognize the raw energy of that music, but their attitudes towards it and their interpretation of the lyrics will differ (lyrics are as vague as they are precisely to allow such multiplicity of personal interpretations) and they may associate the music with different personal recollections.

This also means that there is greater discrepancy between the encoding and the decoding processes. On the one hand, when approaching the series from the production side one can appreciate the careful matching of extracts from the songs to the news events, the balancing of the various strands: a chronology of the year, a catalogue of its important music, and the cross-relations between the two as created by the multimodal sequences. On the other, there is the much more sporadic processing, where moments of meaning may emerge like the tips of icebergs in a sea of drifting images, words and music, such as the already discussed repeated 'mighty Quinn ...' highlighting images of a guitar, a face in the crowd, Dubček, an American flag – images which we must then somehow associate, without ever being told how, so that we are thrown back on our own resources to do so. In this discrepancy between production and reception, *Rock 'n' Roll Years* appeals to the postmodern acceptance of plural and indeterminate texts. Yet the associations, the links and, in the end, the resources on which we draw to make them, are also already potentially provided by the different social and cultural reference points through which we activate some rather than other sets of meanings.

Plurality of viewers

Viewers' reactions, informally gauged at various institutions, showed predictable divergence. Two Eastern European women, both in their fifties, one from Poland and one from the Czech Republic, strongly disapproved of the approach of the programme. They felt it trivialized deeply serious political events. A 40-year-old American, on the other hand, responded enthusiastically ('an excellent tool for understanding the year'), as did a 23-year-old French student ('I think it would have been good to be born twenty years earlier to live in these times'). A group of German students in their mid-twenties, who had until their teens grown up in either East or West Germany, reflected in their comments a similar split, with the former group in particular dismissing the series as deeply trivial. Such responses betray different attitudes to the contemporary mixture of information and entertainment, music and message, personal and political. Traditionally the world of news and current affairs is a world where the truth matters, while music is a world where taste matters. We do not ask whether music is true; we ask whether we like it – we give what we consider to be a personal and emotive response to it. This is by no means true of all societies. Shostakovich was urged by the Soviet culture controllers to make greater use of the major triad in his music to give enduring expression to the heroism of the people's lives in the period of the victory of socialism (Nestyev 1961: 458). In *From Mao to Mozart*, a British documentary about a visit made by Isaac Stern to China, the conductor of the Beijing symphony explains how Mozart expresses the transition from feudalism to the industrial era – and Stern, schooled in another view of music, reels back and exclaims that music and politics have nothing to do with each other. In *Rock 'n' Roll Years* political events move from the world of truth into the world of taste, where emotive identification matters most and debates aiming to reach the truth no longer make sense. It is thus understandable that some question the legitimacy of this approach. How far such questioning goes, meanwhile, varies in accordance with the seriousness of the news events and the amount of irony in the link between song and news event.

The *Rock 'n' Roll Years* approach was found more objectionable when a relatively straightforward, non-ironic commentary accompanied, for instance, pictures of starving children, as when part of the Leonard Cohen song 'Suzanne' was heard below pictures of starving children in Biafra ('There are children in the seaweed, there are children in the morning, they are reaching out for love, and they will reach that way forever'). It was found less objectionable when the issue was less serious, as in the case of the 'Urban space man' song accompanying the *Apollo 8* launch. Witty, ironic or sarcastic comments were approved of most of all, as with Frank Zappa's 'The ugliest part of your body is your mind' behind Enoch Powell's racist speech, or Cilla Black's 'Step inside love' behind pictures of Asian immigrants from Nairobi. The general mood songs, such as the song by the Rolling Stones with the Paris rebellion, caused most divergence, depending almost entirely on people's appreciation of the song itself and on their personal mythology of 1968. The key factors, then, were a concern about the programme's mixture of entertainment music and serious political or humanitarian issues, the strong social stratification of musical taste in our society and differences in attitudes towards the news events which stem from such factors as age and nationality.

Conclusion

This brief discussion of the interaction between popular songs and news items from the same year has focused on a particular instance of a postmodern genre which brings together previously disconnected media texts and combines them into a single form. Our interest was to explore the relationship between the channels of the new combined text, insofar as one can be seen as an encoded commentary on the other, and to highlight the speed and versatility of decoding which the programme expects of its viewers. This complexity may, however, paradoxically be resolved by an overall appeal to nostalgia about the past, which then undercuts the sophistication of the programme's structure and its highly developed parody and subversive detail. There is thus a tension between the complex viewing habit presupposed in the viewers – an ability simultaneously and instantaneously to process information from a range of discrepant verbal, musical and visual flashes – and at the same time a general resolution of these into myth, in Barthes' sense. Unsurprisingly, viewers responded to the programme in highly divergent ways which were partly a result of differences in world knowledge but more significantly a result of the divergent social attitudes, political beliefs and aesthetic preferences of each individual viewer.

Notes

1   We would like to thank Marc Bergman for his help with an earlier draft of this chapter.
2   The following abbreviations are used in the coding of the images:
    CS   close shot, a 'head and shoulders' shot
    MCS   medium close shot, a shot cutting off the human figure at approximately the waist
    MS   medium shot, a shot cutting off the human figure at approximately the knees
    MLS   medium long shot, a shot in which the human figure is shown full length
    LS   long shot, a shot in which the human figure occupies about half the height of the screen
    VCS   very close shot
    Wipe   a shot transition in which a vertical line moves across the shot, pushing one shot out and at the same time dragging the next one in
    'Sync' speech is lip-synchronized with the image (or other sounds with the movements that produce them).

References

Barthes, R. (1973), *Mythologies*, London: Paladin.
Barthes, R. (1977), *Image – Music – Text*, New York: Hill & Wang.
Baudrillard, J. (1988), *Selected Writings*, ed. Mark Poster, Oxford: Polity Press.
Eco, U. (1986), *Travels in Hyperreality*, New York: Harcourt Brace Jovanovich.
Jameson, F. (1984), 'Postmodernism, or the cultural logic of late capitalism', *New Left Review* 146: 53–92.
Jameson, F. (1991), *Postmodernism, or the Cultural Logic of Late Capitalism*, London: Verso.
Kress, G. and van Leeuwen, T. (1996), *Reading Images. The Grammar of Visual Design*, London and New York: Routledge.
Marothy, J. (1974), *Music and the Bourgeois, Music and the Proletarian*, Budapest: Akademiai Kiado.
Meinhof, U. H. (1993), 'Facts, factions, fictions, fakes. Social semiotics and problems of representation', *Social Semiotics* 3.2: 201–17.
Meinhof, U. H. (1994), 'Double encoding in news broadcast', in *Media Texts: Authors and Readers*, eds D. Graddol and O. Boyd-Barrett, Clevedon: Multilingual Matters, 212–23.
Meinhof, U. H. (1998), *Language Learning in the Age of Satellite Television*, Oxford: Oxford University Press.
Nestyev, I. V. (1961), *Prokoviev*, Oxford: Oxford University Press.
van Dijk, T. and W. Kintsch, W. (1983), *Strategies of Discourse Comprehension*, London: Academic Press.
van Leeuwen, T. (1985), 'Rhythmic structure of the film text', in *Discourse and Communication: New Approaches to the Analysis of Mass Media Discourse and Communication*, ed. T. Van Dijk, Berlin: de Gruyter.

5

Intertextuality and the discursive construction of knowledge: the case of economic understanding

KAY RICHARDSON

Introduction

At the University of Liverpool we have been trying to investigate how viewers make sense of TV news when the subject of that news is the national economy. The national economy is a topic which really does challenge both broadcasters and viewers. On the one hand, it is deemed to be of central importance to modern democratic states, even as national autonomy in economic affairs becomes subject to erosion. On the other hand, it is a topic of considerable complexity, where the significance of, for example, a rise in the rate of inflation, has to be contextualized in relation to other economic 'indicators' and the implications of the rise – which may be contested – have to be explained. The relations between national economic discourse and other public discourses (politics, international relations) must also be attended to.

The significance of this research in the present context is as follows. It is our belief that economic knowledge is highly dependent upon the mass media. For good or for ill, what people know or think they know about the state of the national economy is derived in large measure from what the newspaper and broadcast journalists say about it, drawing upon the perspectives of relevant participants such as politicians, financial experts, interest groups and even 'ordinary people'. This is not to argue that the mass media is the only source of economic understanding and information, only that it is a place where economic affairs are drawn into a 'national' matrix and rendered 'public'. Thus, the context which produced our research data is an ineluctably 'intertextual' one. I propose in this chapter to use the concept of intertextuality in an exploration of what it means for ordinary people to present themselves as knowing something – however little – about the national economy. The research which will permit me to do this involved the use of focus groups responding to short extracts of broadcast TV news of an economic character. The research groups can be seen as engaged in the discursive construction of knowledgeability through the deployment of intertextually derived 'information' embedded within the matrices of their own understandings. It is a familiar principle within media research that textual 'meanings' are not fixed, but produced in the negotiation between text and audience (for recent relevant work, see References, p. 97).

The nature of our research design allowed the respondents, within their groups, to present themselves as 'knowing subjects'. The research design itself was straightforward enough: short extracts were chosen by us from current broadcast material and compiled into a dub tape. Within two weeks of the original broadcast, the dub tape would be screened to selected respondents, who attended the research sessions as focus groups. Our focus groups had an occupational character, and the research took place over three 'rounds', during the winter of 1995/6, with different extracts in each round. Four core groups (sixth formers, garage workers, librarians and Rotary Club businessmen) participated in each round and other groups (including theatre workers, hospital auxiliary staff, undergraduate students, Church of England workers, university cleaners) participated either in round 2 or round 3.

In saying that this research design allowed respondents to represent themselves as 'knowing subjects', I am attempting to draw attention to the spirit in which the discussions of the dub tape were conducted. As researchers we had an agenda of concerns about TV's economic discourse. We were concerned of course with its 'density' of information. But we were also interested in its use of varying formal and communicative strategies to manage that information, and the rationale for these, as well as appreciating the kinds of criteria that the broadcasters felt that they had to satisfy – to be accessible, to do justice to controversy, to relate economic news to viewers' own lives, to acknowledge the perspectives of different 'sectors' of the economy. We sought to explore all of these issues through the questions that we asked respondents to discuss immediately after the screenings. The research setting did not generate 'ordinary conversation' about the news, nor was it intended to. Instead, it gave the groups space and opportunity to go into detail about their reactions to the screened material. And in inviting this kind of talk, we were of course also providing opportunities for 'presentations of self' appropriate to this task to be developed. One aspect of this presentation, encouraged by the forms of the questions asked, was a focus upon knowledgeability, both about the economy and about television.

A preliminary conclusion from the research data is that respondents do have knowledge about the national economy, knowledge which they have appropriated as 'theirs' in the sense that they reproduce it without acknowledgement and with high modality, using it in causal reasoning to derive conclusions which they can present as their own opinion. In Example 1 below, the absence of growth, the existence of a national debt and the 'unemployment problem' is the knowledge which warrants the conclusion that it is going to be hard for the country to get out of its 'problems'. The speaker is a sixth-form student, one of the youngest participants in the research.

Example 1

> Respondent: It seems to me that we're ... it's died somewhat [the economy]. There's no growth whatsoever and we're just stuck now trying to pay off all our debts before we even start. And with the unemployment problem, I can't see any way of us getting out of the sort of problems that we've got, let alone ... let alone starting to grow again.
> *Sixth formers, round 1*

A second conclusion is that respondents' knowledge is limited, and felt to be so by them, though their difficulties of understanding and lack of information are rather readily acknowledged, which suggests that very little shame attaches to 'ignorance' and comprehension failure in this area, as in the following examples.

Example 2

> Respondent: Figures? I didn't understand most of it. And for me to give you an informed comment on what I thought about it is going to be quite hard because I didn't think a great deal ... I didn't understand all of what he was saying. I'm not really a pupil of economics and that sort of thing and I found that difficult to understand. And a couple of times I had to say: come on, think now cos you're going to be asked questions about this. Listen to it. Cos I was wandering, you know? It wasn't easy to understand. Whether that's Peter Jay or whether it's the way they had the figures and the graphs and whatever on the screen, I don't know. But I didn't like this at all.
> *Rotarians, round 2*

Example 3

> Respondent: I mean, a lot of it ... I mean, public expenditure and all that, it's just, like, phrases I don't really understand. They're showing you billions of pounds on little figures in the bottom right-hand corner and all: point-three per cent of this and point-three per cent of that. I mean, means nothing to me.
> *Garage workers, round 1*

Example 4

> Respondent 1:   Well I find ... I find the whole subject – economy – quite hard to understand.
> Respondent 2:   Yeah.
> Respondent 3:   Yeah. Some of the terms used. Like, there was the something deficit.
> Respondent 1:   Deficit, yeah.
> Respondent 3:   Err ... What was it? The something deficit, and I didn't understand what it was. So then I couldn't follow the next few minutes cos they were talking about it. And cos I didn't know what the deficit was, I couldn't, like, understand what they were talking about. So ... some terms that they used. I mean, I'm not saying they had to use, like, you know, just these terms you can't understand but, like, if you don't know what they mean then you can't really follow, you know, what they're talking about.
> *Sixth formers, round 2*

Example 5

> Respondent 1:   I did find it easier cos I've always wondered what,
> you know, the borrowing deficit is, and government borrowing and
> that. So it did make it a bit clearer – the little graph that ... it said,
> you know, the difference between the revenue and ... is it the
> deficit or whatever. I did find it clearer on the graph, yeah.
> Respondent 2:   So, I mean, they're difficult issues to start with, so
> you can make it as clear as you can and it's still quite difficult to
> understand.
> Respondent 3:   It's very difficult to follow when they start talking
> about government deficits and borrowing and targets and projec-
> tions because you're not sure really what they mean.
> *Library workers, round 2*

The interest of Example 2 lies in the fact that it is spoken by a member of the Rotary Club group. The Rotarians collectively expressed considerable knowledge about economic affairs, which they followed principally in relation to their own business interests. The sentiment here is one reproduced in all the groups but its occurrence in this educated and well-informed group was particularly noteworthy. The point is that this kind of admission can be incorporated within the discourse of the knowing subject. It takes a particular kind of subjectivity, the same kind in each case, both to 'possess' knowledge and to acknowledge those limitations of knowledge which make comprehension problematic.

As originally planned the research was designed to explore how people made sense of TV news when the subject of the news broadcast had an economic character. It was not designed to explore, using TV, what people knew and understood about the economy. The distinction is an important one because the former emphasis focuses much more upon television and its devices of communication than upon the conditions of knowledge. The latter emphasis would require a different approach and one designed with much more attention to the range of sources that people use in constructing a usable 'knowledge base' – personal experience, formal education, social networks, the press, radio, books. Nevertheless, the data gathered for the TV research does speak to the 'knowledge' agenda, provided that it is approached in an appropriate way. In the first place it is necessary to adopt a particular perspective upon the relationship between the screened dub tape and the ensuing discussion. It can of course be seen as an object to be 'understood', or not, by the respondent groups, and that was how we mainly intended it. But it can also be seen as a device to facilitate a particular kind of talk, with a grounding in economic affairs. In the first place, it undoubtedly gave the groups something to talk about, so that, for example, exophoric references to 'the baker' were immediately comprehensible to all group members including researchers. 'The baker' was an interviewee in our first screened extract, a location report from Bristol with a baker as a token small trader. Example 6 reproduces both the original statement from the broadcast and one respondent's reference to it.

Example 6

> Text: Wilton's Bakery has served the Fishponds Road area of Bristol on this spot for over 100 years. The oven, which bakes the loaves and cakes, is almost as old, and the skills of the staff are even more traditional. Weddings, birthdays and Christmas still come in the toughest economic times, but the baker can't remember a tougher time.
> *BBC, Peter Jay, 15 Nov. 1995*
> Respondent: It's that bad the baker's got to make one of his staff unemployed. About redundancy and the like. It all goes back to the high street, doesn't it.
> *Garage workers, round 1*

In the second place, the exposure to these taped TV news extracts helped to activate the 'background knowledge' most relevant to the topic. This did not always prevent respondents digressing into other areas (especially politics) but it did provide a sense of context and appropriacy, and, as suggested, pulling 'forward' into consciousness information that might otherwise have remained latent.

Levels of intertextuality

The primary text for the purposes of this exercise is the (taped and transcribed) discussion within the respondent group. Inevitably, the talk which ensues in this context reaches out beyond the immediate here-and-now of the encounter – and its intertextual profile is one which can usefully be examined in terms of three levels. First-level ıality can be seen as the level which, within the discussion, references to the extracts which the respondents have just s part of the research process. Second-level intertextuality involves references to other specified sources of information. Third-level intertextuality weakens the specificity of the references down to particular kinds of sources such as 'politicians' or 'experts'. The limited case of third-level intertextuality involves no specification of a source. In the sections to follow I will elaborate upon this provisional typology, which, although devised in order to make sense of the research data, may prove to have its uses, suitably adapted, in other contexts.

First-level intertextuality

First-level intertextuality in this context involves references produced by the respondents to the extracts they have just viewed as part of the research fieldwork. These references come in two forms, broadly speaking. Since, for every extract screened (there were nine such extracts altogether) we asked respondents what points they thought the item was making, it is not surprising that they produced a range of summary or 'gist' statements about the meaning or point of the item screened, along the following lines. These quotations (Example 7, Example 8 and Example 9) are from different groups, responding to different items.

Example 7

> Interviewer: Just to start very generally, what do you think the main points that story was making were?
> Respondent: I think if anything they were trying to make a point about unemployment creeping back up again.
> *Garage workers, round 1*

Example 8

> Interviewer: I want to ask again what do you think were the main points of this story? ...
> Respondent: Tax cuts. About lowering people's ... Tax cuts and interest rates for the vote, for the budget.
> *Librarians, round 1*

Example 9

> Interviewer: OK. So what are the main points that that little item's making?
> Respondent: The government are reducing ... reducing the amount that they spend on their departments and using that money that they've saved to reduce taxes.
> *Sixth formers, round 1*

First-level intertextuality occurs also in the form of specific references to textual details from the screened extracts, serving different purposes at different moments of the talk. In Example 10 the respondents are discussing the merits of an extract which seeks to explore the extent of economic well-being in Britain by concentrating not on areas of poverty and deprivation but on 'the heart of England'. The subjects interviewed are represented as economically anxious.

Example 10

> Interviewer: So is there a sense in which, perhaps, these weren't a representative group even of Tory voters in a small town?
> Respondent: No, they seemed to be a fairly good idea of what a Tory person is. Do you know what I mean? They were middle-class people, owned their own homes, and, like, they're worrying about all the ... They can't sell their houses cos the market's down, you know.
> *Garage workers, round 2*

One of the differences between reading for detail and reading for gist is the presence of different 'they's. In referring to details, 'they' may well have an explicit antecedent in the respondents' own talk or that of the researchers, but whether it does or not there is always an unambiguous referent in the original screened extracts. Above, the referent of 'they' is the selection of families presented in the extract who talk about their personal circumstances, but glossed first in the discussion as 'Tory voters': 'That was like an independent news team asking Tories about Tories', says one respondent, asked to say what the item was about.

When offering a 'gist' or summary interpretation, a different kind of 'they' is called into play – an authorial 'they'.

Example 11

> Interviewer: Just to start very generally, what do you think the main points that story was making were?
> Respondent: I think if anything they were trying to make a point about unemployment creeping back up again.
> *Garage workers, round 1*

It would be a mistake to take this as a reference only to the broadcasters who appear on-screen – the studio presenter and the location reporter. It has a much looser relation to the text-as-screened, and shows that the respondents do indeed recognize the broadcasts as authored texts with specific communicational purposes. Usages of this kind become commoner still when respondents allow themselves to speculate upon the reasons why the extract is as it is.

Example 12

> Respondent: They mentioned tax which, basically ... which affects the general public generally, and they mentioned interest rates which will affect business generally. I got the feeling they were just trying to cover a wider spectrum.
> *Rotarians, round 1*

'They' is a word with several functions in this talk. Because of the way that the textual context is constructed, the usages I have illustrated so far do not necessarily require textual antecedents within the talk itself. Frequently, our respondents rely upon first-level intertextuality to take care of the meaning – as well they might, in a context which has been shared by all participants, including the researchers.

First-level intertextuality and the credibility problem

The talk of respondents in their discussion groups revolves around the text-extracts they have seen and therefore involves a fairly constant flow of first-level intertextuality, punctuated by references out to the broader knowledge domain as well as digressions on related topics. At all levels of intertextuality respondents embed the propositions of economic discourse within utterances modalized to indicate appropriate degrees of confidence or scepticism. At the first level of intertextuality, for example, there is much opportunity to register the content of the broadcast material in propositional terms: to react to broadcasters themselves (studio presenters, economic editors and other correspondents) as well as to the sources whose views are presented on camera (politicians, experts, sectional representatives, ordinary people). Any economic proposition is vulnerable to the 'sceptical reading' which puts the utterance of it in brackets as something heard but not yet taken on board as factual: 'He would say that, wouldn't he'. Such propositions are also vulnerable to a range of other questioning strategies. They are likely, for example, to be challenged as to their *relevance* within the world in which their impact is supposed to lie. It will be helpful to examine a range of 'first-level' examples to establish this point.

Example 13

> Respondent: Seems to be a bit of a conflict of interest between the chancellor – he's saying that we'll cut this base rate to sort of stimulate the economy – and yet they were saying that banks and building societies aren't going to act upon it. And I thought, well, it's just a bit in limbo now, isn't it? It's sort of what is the point of doing all this? And the average person watching that sort of clip would probably think, well, what are they playing at? What are they trying to do? What are we going to get from this? Which seems to be virtually nothing. So it seems again as if they're just bandying things around and there'll sort of be ... there's nothing concrete coming from it.
> *Library workers, round 3*

Example 14

> Respondent: So, I mean, I don't see what difference it's going to make if the banks and the building societies aren't going to pass that on anyway.
> *Sixth formers, round 3*

Example 15

> Respondent: Well, I don't think that is strictly true. I don't think a quarter of a per cent change or half a per cent on the interest rate affects the man or lady in the street one iota.
> *Rotarians, round 3*

Example 16

> Respondent: I can't understand why they said there was a quarter of a per cent cut and they're not passing it on, what the point is of them telling us ...
> Respondent: It must affect the money market which is where the government deals heavy in it, isn't it? But, I mean, I don't understand how it does. Well above my head, you know.
> *Garage workers, round 3*

All of these examples are reactions to a news item reporting a small reduction in the Bank of England interest rate – the base rate, set by the government. In recent times the base rate had featured in economic news as a point of tension between Eddie George, the governor of the Bank of England, and Kenneth Clark, the chancellor of the exchequer. The latter, putting faith in the power of lower interest rates to encourage economic growth, looked to reduce interest rates when he was able to, whilst the former, with low inflation as his chief priority, sought to resist cuts in the base rate or even to urge its increase.

Example 13 shows the respondent's understanding of the logic which drives the chancellor's policy; he notes the further information that the building societies and high-street banks have decided not to reduce their own interest rates, and wonders therefore if the exercise was worthwhile. How does this compare with the responses in the other three groups?

Across all four groups our respondents try to tell us that there is little 'point' in this piece of economic news. And yet they are all thinking along slightly different lines. In Example 16, though the speaker believes that there is little point in treating the base-rate cut as newsworthy (a criticism of the broadcasters), there probably is a 'point' to the chancellor's action itself. However, that point is at a level of economic life that the respondent does not understand and was given no help with by the extract. In three cases the policy itself is seen as rather 'pointless', as regards its impact upon ordinary people, either because it is such a small percentage cut (one quarter of one per cent – Example 15) or because the banks and building societies are not planning to implement a cut on their own account (Example 14), or quite possibly both (Example 13). These are not criticisms of the broadcasters, directly, but of the policy makers.

The differences of emphasis in the accounts given by the respondents are interesting because they begin to show how individuals might move from specific judgements on particular cases to more general ones (which may obscure the lower-level differences). There is important research to be done upon how people feel about the relations between economic life on the one hand and economic policy-making/politics on the other hand. It may well be that people increasingly regard politicians as impotent to act upon the realities of economic life (politicians sometimes have an interest in fostering this view in certain respects). Certainly, Example 13 can be taken as an expression of just such a sentiment. However, it is still not common in economic discourse: the chancellor on budget day and the treasury teams of both front benches continue to talk as if policy-making mattered; the broadcasters continue to report the discourse of politicians and in their own reportage to reproduce the significance of politics: it is hardly surprising if, most of the time, our respondents likewise understand that policies make a difference. Even their complaints here about the 'pointlessness' of this particular economic measure carry the implication that more could have been done by a less timid chancellor or one less trapped by other pressures. Sometimes the perplexity surrounding what government can or cannot do will emerge explicitly.

Example 17

> Respondent: The very last thing at the end of the article was, like, the chancellor feels the economy needs a boost so he can cut, like, a quarter or half a per cent. I mean, why not cut a full per cent off and give it even more of a boost, you know? I ... It's beyond me, the way they can talk like that.
> *Garage workers, round 2*

Example 18

> Respondent: And I cynically look at these graphs they're showing us running in credit in the year 2000. My same cynicism comes over as me in a small business cos the chancellor's running a big business, I run a small business, but it's still money management. And between now and the year 2000, there could be another oil crisis, there could be a great development that suddenly finds a way of running motor cars on water, there could be ... Something will come into the machine that stops what he's predicting to happen.
> *Rotarians, round 2*

Example 19

> Respondent: Well, the reporter seemed to think that – and the people who were speaking seemed to think that – everything that he [said] was predicted, as though all his figures would work out. Everything seemed to be very optimistic, hoping the interest rates will stay low and the inflation will stay low and the exports will go up massively at the same time. It all seems a bit hopeful.
> *Sixth formers, round 2*

Example 20

> Respondent: It just seemed very vague. It was like he had all these plans for the future that nobody really knows exactly what they are, how they're going to be achieved. And it just seems very woolly, you know.
> *Library workers, round 2*

The dilemmas here revolve around what the government does have power to do (raise taxes, set borrowing targets), what it can only aim for (achieve the borrowing targets, create full employment) and what it can only predict (growth rates). As the foregoing examples show, the knowledgeability of respondents has taken these dilemmas on board, although not with the sophistication of some TV economic reportage. Notorious in this regard is Peter Jay, the BBC's economics editor, who, during the period of our research, was given fairly regular opportunities to survey the national economic scene. Here is an example of his style of commentary, from one of the dub

tapes screened to our respondents. It is not the full text of J[
report, merely the concluding section.

Example 21

> The big puzzle about today is how the chancellor has managed to forecast such rapid economic growth while professing to introduce a neutral budget. Part of the answer may lie in plans to slash interest rates and part certainly lies in great optimism about exports. Another part may lie in the chancellor's belief that the increased budget deficits will boost the economy, while he prefers not to say so for fear of upsetting the financial markets. All that assumes that he hasn't decided that the way to win the next election is the way they won the last one – in a recession.
> *BBC news, 28 Nov. 1995*

Second-level intertextuality

Second-level intertextuality generates references to other extra-textual sources of information, of such a kind that the text in question could if necessary be recovered and analysed in its own right. Second-level intertextuality came into this research in an obvious way during the second and the third screening rounds with the core groups of garage workers, library workers, Rotarians and sixth formers, since they remembered things from the earlier screening rounds and would refer to them in a comparative way from time to time – though not very much. The next example, from the second screening round, features the baker from Bristol featured in the first round.

Example 22

> Respondent 1:   Yeah, I mean ... there was a ... saucepan factory from Burnley, you know.
> Respondent 2:   Yeah, the saucepan factory.
> Respondent 1:   That's like the baker from Bristol, you know ...
> *Sixth formers, round 2*

In examples like this, respondents show their appreciation of functional similarities across the texts, at the level of generic form.

Overall there was very little second-level intertextuality of this kind, very little by way of reference to specific sources. A rare example is given in Example 23. (The comment about Granada's take-over bid for Forte was not particularly germane to the course of discussion and was not subsequently pursued.)

Example 23

> Respondent: What you were saying Alisdair is that you pick out things in the morning that you ... In the morning, my radio comes on automatically. I love the stock market news: what figures are going to be released today and ... Especially retail figures and ... who's taking ... who's having a go at who, like Granada is having a go at Forte and ... And I thought, I thought this morning, oh, I can't see that happening. Forte's? You know what I mean, you know? I can't see ... That family, I can't see them caving in to Granada. Not me. But I'm always interested in that, every morning.
> *Rotarians, round 1*

Our respondent here is not explicit in indicating to the group which radio show on which channel told him about the take-over bid that morning, but the missing information is all in principle recoverable and there is little doubt that there was a particular announcement at a particular time on a particular show – general knowledge suggests the *Today* programme on Radio Four.

There are of course general references to the importance of the TV news, the radio news, specific programmes such as the *Money Programme*, the greater depth of coverage found in newspapers, etc., but such comments are usually made in a global way without reference to any specific item learned from any specific source.

Before moving on to talk about third-level intertextuality, I want to say something about Example 24 in terms of the model which I am trying to develop, since it operates as a kind of intermediate form between second- and third-level intertextuality.

Example 24

> Respondent: But the economy is still in a really bad state cos look at the way they're fighting for business. You walk down the high street now and there's constant sales on. It used to be like there's a

sale in January and a sale, like, summertime. Now everywhere you go there's always sales on somewhere. Isn't there, like, really a lot of sales? Like, they seem to be fighting for the business really.
Sixth formers, round 1

Central cases of intertextuality will always be those where the reference is to a *specific* text or other source. This is not such a case. An argument is being presented (that the national economy is in a bad state) and a certain kind of evidence is used in justification of that argument. The evidence is 'experiential', and the experience is semiotic-textual. It is also, importantly, *quantitative* – the speaker's point is that 'sales' all year round is evidence of problems in the retail trade. Hence the reference to the semiotic experience of sales in the high street is necessarily not to any single text, but to their – excessive – plurality. The shift from singularity to plurality a shift from second- to third-level intertextuality.

Third-level intertextuality

Intertextuality of the third level generates further levels of engagement with economic discourse. This is the level which allows us some insight into the ways in which respondents derive their knowledge and understanding of public affairs in general and the national economy in particular. One way of thinking about this is in relation to the observation that 'knowledge' in our culture has a way of presenting itself as *decontextualized*. Information can be free-standing, that is, detached from the situation of utterance, whether that be in written or spoken form. All information is encountered in some context or other, but when the context becomes irrelevant that information can be said to have taken on a life of its own. 'There's no growth', said one respondent, and another: 'I think it's increased slightly a couple of years ago, and then they increased taxes and other things, and that's sort of had a downward spiral on the economy', relating 'fact' (increased taxes) to 'opinion' (economic decline) in an unexceptionable way.

But it is not always easy for information to pass through the filter of scepticism into the respondents' own knowledge base, with the result that propositions about the economy live a kind of half-life, enclosed within inverted commas. It is this arena of inverted commas that I want to characterize as third-level intertextuality, extensions of the 'pluralized' second-level intertextuality that I discussed in the previous section. Respondents are very aware of the circulation of propositions about the economy. They are often aware in a general way of the sources from which those propositions emanate. This understanding allows them to be confident in re-presenting those propositions, but not in reproducing them as their own beliefs or knowledge. Attribution to other voices is a useful modality for distancing economic truth-claims, where they have to be distanced because of the difficulty of processing such complex material or because economic claims are so often contested. Indeed, the point of such a quotative strategy is often to draw attention to the difficulty of believing information which is contested, or revised too often, or emanates from less than fully trustworthy sources. In some cases a generalized source is registered in the talk ('politicians' in Example 25) whilst in other cases there is no such indication (as in Example 26).

Example 27 deploys a memory of the kind of things that politicians used to say, whilst Example 28 challenges political assertion with personal conviction.

Example 25

> Respondent: The recession. They always seem to be talking about that, like. Whether we're coming out of it – one year they say we are, then they say we're not.
> *Sixth formers, round 1*

Example 26

> Respondent: To be honest, I find it very difficult to decide how it is going because you've got one set of politicians saying we're doing marvellously well and everything's fine, and on the other hand they're saying no, it's not, it's the worst position we've been in for nine, ten years. So you really don't know.
> *Library workers, round 1*

Example 27

> Respondent: You had it ... I mean, you go back to the '50s and
> '60s and you got people like Macmillan and Wilson and they used to
> talk about housing starts each year, the number of housing starts
> there were. And that was the barometer of the economy – how
> many houses have we built compared to the number of houses you
> built? And that never even enters into any political discussion now in
> the '90s.
> *Rotarians, round 1*

Example 28

> Respondent: I think we're just floundering on recession, basically,
> even though we were told we were coming out of it.
> *Garage workers, round 1*

The things 'they' say can also be rendered in the talk as the
things 'we' and 'you' hear.

Example 29

> Respondent: Well, this is what you hear, week in, week out, reces-
> sion, recession, recession, and as I said before I don't see any signs
> of it out there.
> *Garage workers, round 1*

Example 30

> Respondent: Well, if you look over the last eighteen years and the
> amount of jobs that the country's lost. I mean, we keep hearing this
> market forces strategy. What happened to industry? We import coal-
> mining. We import other things. There's no cotton trade anymore,
> no coal trade.
> *Garage workers, round 2*

Example 31

Interviewer: Mmm, right. OK. Did you find the ... I mean, insofar as they covered the issues, did you find it easy to understand? Was it fairly sort of transparent? Was it fairly easy to get a grip on?
Respondent: Well, it was something that we already ... you know, we already had a lot of ... I mean, we've been hearing the likes of this for the last few years. And it's gradually gone more miserable over the period of time, you know.
Garage workers, round 3 (reacting to an 'optimistic' story about the economy)

Example 32

Interviewer: When you hear that word, what kinds of things does it bring into your mind? What does it make you think of?
...
Respondent: The budget and inflation and interest rates. It's all terms I've heard of but I don't really understand them.
Sixth formers, round 1

Example 33

Respondent: I mean, out in the street you hear people always complaining but on the news you do hear the odd story about unemployment falling.
Sixth formers, round 1

Example 34

Respondent: You hear about loads of companies making millions and millions of pounds each year and yet they're still making people redundant as well.
Sixth formers, round 1

Example 35

> Respondent: Cos it was a day after, I mean, one day you heard that it's ... it's all depression – nothing was getting really better – and then, next day it's: oh, it's all right, you know – everything's OK.
> *Sixth formers, round 1*

Example 36

> Respondent: You hear about a lot of new businesses going bust in the first eighteen months, don't you?
> *Sixth formers, round 3*

Example 37

> Respondent: I just think that most of the stuff I've heard about the budget's been based on how much more you've got to pay for a packet of cigarettes and beer and petrol, and I haven't really picked up anything of the major issues about the economy at all.
> *Geography students, round 2*

Conclusions

Have I written a chapter about the presentation of self in a research discussion, or one about economic knowledge and understanding? I hope that it is a contribution under both of these headings. In respect of presentation of self, I have shown how TV audience members or ordinary people work through their encounters with the screening material, their life-world experiences and the fragments of their textual formations, to produce a very particular kind of talk, in which their knowledgeability can be displayed and managed.

Under the heading of economic knowledge and understanding, I have attempted to foreground the ability which most respondents undoubtedly have, to relate economic propositions (facts) to more general conclusions, whilst handling those 'facts' with a certain amount of caution. Yet under this heading there is certainly more

to be done. What is missing here is any *substantive* account of
ses to which this ability is put. Future work, by the team at the
University of Liverpool or by others, will certainly have to attend to
this issue, by asking such questions as these: Which are the sources
that are doubted by respondents and which are the trusted? How
far does their understanding of what the national government can
control correspond with the government's own rhetorical stance on
this point (or with the opposition's stance, for that matter)? What
forms of TV presentation carry the most authority? Which are the
most comprehensible? Is the rhetoric of 'national interest' one
which influences all respondents, or do they have ways of position-
ing themselves 'outside' this supposed consensus framework?

Finally, a theoretical point. The use of the term 'intertextuality'
in modern semiotics and critical theory arose in the context of literary research, and is associated with (among others) the names of
Julia Kristeva and Roland Barthes, both of whom were keen to find
a way past the traditional focus upon 'the author' as the source of
literary meaning. Certainly it is now true that in many areas of
cultural research, including media studies, 'the author' has been
displaced as the originary source of meaning. It is not controversial
to describe texts as assemblages of textual and semiotic fragments,
and to play down the extent of the author's conscious and deliberate control over the processes of collection and assembly. This
approach to the construction of meaning has been extended, quite
rightly, beyond the domain of literary production; it has also been
accompanied by an increasing emphasis upon the functions of
readers/listeners as participants in the construction of meaning,
thus placing an even greater question mark over the unity of 'the
text'.

The utility of this perspective when approaching aspects of
meaning which do not aspire to *literary* value is a concern of other
chapters in this book besides my own. It is an important question.
When, for example, media messages are viewed non-semiotically as
carriers of 'content' – as in mainstream American media research
within social-scientific paradigms – it is not obvious that there is or
ever has been a problem to which a desacralized notion of 'text'
would be the answer. 'Content', in this sense, was never viewed as
originating within the particular objects operationalized as the data-
base for quantification. I am not advocating a return to a
non-semiotic view of communication, only suggesting that the

reified 'text' was perhaps more of a problem *within* literary/semiotic analysis than outside of it.

In attempting to extend the concept of intertextuality into an exploration of what it is that people 'know', how they process propositional content and incorporate it into their talk about the national economy and its representation on television, I am conscious of trying to push that concept into an area it was never designed to address. The danger of course is of trying to force a marriage between semiotic analysis and something much more positivist in its assumptions – of trying to reconcile approaches to media analysis which are epistemologically incompatible. But I believe it is a risk worth taking, and that it is possible to analyse propositional knowledge as part of the projection of self in talk without challenging the significance of that knowledge as the basis of conceptual understanding.

References

Cunningham, S., and Jacka, E., (1997), 'Neighbourly relations? Cross-cultural reception analysis and Australian soaps in Britain', in A. Sreberny-Mohammadi, Dwayne Winseck, Jim McKenna and Oliver Boyd-Barrett (eds), *Media in Global Context: a Reader*, London: Edward Arnold, pp. 299–310.

Gillespie, M. (1995), *Television, Ethnicity and Cultural Change*, London: Routledge.

Gavin, N. *et al.* (eds) (1998), *The Economy, Media and Public Knowledge*, London: University of Leicester Press.

Philo, G. (1990), *Seeing and Believing: The Influence of Television*, London: Routledge.

6

Intertextuality and situative contexts in game shows: the case of *Wheel of Fortune*

LOTHAR MIKOS AND HANS J. WULFF

Skovmand postulates in one of the few available analyses of *Wheel of Fortune* that game shows 'seem not innovative at all, but part of an unbroken and unproblematic historical continuum of cultural practices' (1992: 84). Shows aren't well-informed texts in a narrow sense, but are rather records of social events. Their live quality indicates that they involve more a series of events which unfold in the present than one that has been minutely planned (see Skovmand 1992: 85). This model is of great consequence for an intertextual analysis. A show can be examined less as a series of works, genres, literary topoi, etc., than as 'a field of *cultural practices* which are not necessarily communicated by way of television at all, a field of practices which include parlour games, bingo, fairs, and gossip' (Skovmand 1992: 86; cf. 101).

We would like to propose in this chapter, in keeping with the performance character of game shows, a concept of 'situativity' as a constitutive element of a show's communication. Furthermore, we will show how in the specific example of *Wheel of Fortune* a circle of intertextual (or intersituative) references unfolds and influences the scope of meaning.

Situativity, scene setting and narrative roles

The *situativity* of television texts is to be understood in two ways. On the one hand, the television text is located in a communicative situation. It is always structurally open and geared towards the spectator and necessarily includes both speaker and audience. On the other hand, it reflects certain qualities of the situation all by itself and is bound up in a situative framework.

Using the example of game shows in general, and *Wheel of Fortune* in particular, what follows will examine these two aspects. We understand plot-dominated game shows such as this one to be *social situations*. Their episodes, in turn, depict and dramatize social situations. Thus, a *network of situative frameworks* is produced, from which all those involved in the interaction can orientate their actions. This inclusive definition of the situation affects all roles in the show (host, assistants, guests, players, studio audience and the spectators in front of their televisions).

Television's institutional structure provides the widest framework within which game-show participants – in whatever capacity – behave. Its framework, which can also be referred to as a 'media constellation', provides the 'pre-formatting of communicative roles in a technical dispositive such as television' (Wulff 1993: 121). The situative framework is of varying importance for those taking part in the game. While the network's institutional make-up is surely of no great interest to the players, game-show hosts (similar to talk-show hosts) must always bear the network's conditions and normative markers in mind. These are effective solely by virtue of the fact that the event takes place within television's institutional sphere.

Television's institutional make-up manifests itself in numerous phatic acts – for example, some communications-oriented ethical agreements. Nevertheless, the programme's drawing power, which exists by simple virtue of the fact that it is broadcast, becomes especially pronounced in the case of a scandal. Hosts also act as representatives of the 'institutional order'. They cannot simply ignore a scandal provoked by a guest if it violates the network's ground-rules, and thereby possibly give the broadcasting board grounds for censuring the programme. Programme moderation must live up to institutional demands. The numerous rhetorical references of hosts in variety shows to the fact that one is, in fact, taking part in a show whose only aim is to entertain, can also be understood as a reference to the television framework. The construction of the medium as a medium of entertainment is thereby thematized.

Situative movements are constantly depicted within the general framework of programming, as well as within individual programmes. This extends from programme announcements, to talk shows, to the broadcasting of fictional broadcasting-types.

Broadcasting-types and genres each constitute their own situation which in turn provides the players with a particular situative framework (Mikos 1994a: 138ff.). Therefore, a studio or theatre situation is staged in which the on-stage participants act within the show's generic-situative framework and perform in concrete episodic situations. Each active situation not only occurs in front of the camera, but for the camera. Thus, this thought process always involves a situation which takes place in front of an audience. In staging the show, those in front of the camera interact using each other, the camera and the spectator in front of the screen at home as reference points.

The all-encompassing show situation is broken down into individual episodes which each carry their own situational characteristics. Games and discussions are the most common episodic types of show. However, many other forms are possible and are implemented on a case-by-case basis.

Thus, a show forms a network of three integrated situative frameworks. They are located within the context of television, belong to the genre of television entertainment and include on-stage presentations of individual scenes. As in Habermas (1988: 194), each of these situations or more precisely, situational levels form a set of connections of lifeworld references. Each of these situations defines the framework for possible further communicative behaviour. The behaviour of all show participants can be seen not only as situation management but also as a situative framework in communicative terms.

The show's situative components are of thematic, interpretive and motivational importance to the participants in defining behavioural roles, estimating behavioural possibilities and recognizing the communicative power of each individual actor. What happens in the show is not freely negotiated, but widely set and routinized. The themes are provided as they are defined by both the total show situation and the game situations staged in the individual episodes.

The rules of the game serve clearly to define the situation for the participants (host or master of ceremonies, players, guests). Those who participate in shows generally know what they are in for, and know that they are taking part in a game. Whoever does not, because he or she does not like it, is unable to conform. He or she is excluded from the game and thereby remains barred from communication. The participants' aims need to coincide neither with the aims of the game nor with those of the host. What counts is not only winning, but also having fun.

The players can move within the situative context of the staging with relative ease. They may rely on the fact that the rules of the game will be observed, and that the sequence of activity will be routinized. Room for manoeuvre is nevertheless maintained. *Wheel of Fortune* is an example of actors acting counter to narrow role definition as determined exclusively by the rules of the game. The actors are competitors, according to the definition of the game. At the same time, the game is, broadly speaking, 'a participatory game' (Skovmand 1992: 89). This is expressed when players comfort each other when they have drawn a bad number and celebrate with each other when it is clear who has won. Clearly, the players have the power to determine their behaviour amongst themselves, and thereby act counter to the principle of competition. Although they remain within the framework of the 'game', they draw out the playful quality of the encounter with spontaneous remarks, and determine their own balance between the competitive element and that of 'comradeship' (Skovmand 1992: 90). It is 'only a game' and the true purpose is not material gain but the common pleasure derived from social interaction.

Becoming an actor in a show situation is contingent upon the fulfilment of requirements drawn directly from everyday knowledge. The situations on which individual episodes and games are based are particularly familiar to the players from their own everyday experience. Knowledge of the conventions of the television-show genre, of the schemata of games separate from the shows, of the world in general – all are expressed in the communicative processes that the players use to master the show situation. The actors would be unable to realize the show situation as a behavioural framework without this knowledge.

A show contains an implicit *definition of the situation*. This means that people act according to how they see (or define) a situation. A social situation is only realized when it is configured by its participants as a 'meaningful construct': a framework in which 'meaningful' behaviour is possible. This means that for situational analysis, external behaviour must be applied to the model of meaning which forms the conditional framework for behaviour. A web of social relationships arise from a show that is geared towards everyday situations. Situational analysis is the description of *situative and social meanings* expressed or exhibited in behaviour.

If the construction of the show's situative framework is stereotypical; if behavioural roles form a system in which all partial roles are defined with respect to one another; if the concrete order of a show is routinized and takes place within a framework of predictable rules and norms, then conditions are present within which the emotional climate of security and familiarity can shelter individual behaviour. Participation in a staged show situation becomes an everyday act within a familiar everyday situation. The host, assistants, players and audience in the studio have faith in the conditions of the communicative constellation. This faith forms the behavioural background for all those involved in the game show. As the rules of the game provide for winners and losers, disappointment after a lost game is limited. The players know that winning and losing are basic elements of games. The trust the players place in the host is essentially constituted as a basic sense of trust in the rules and norms of the show, and not in terms of personal trust. The players do not need to feel as if they have been attacked personally if the host falls out of 'character'. This character break can be interpreted as a transgression of the show's rules by the host. It can be countered by referring back to these rules and norms. Faith in the rules and norms of the show situation is faith in the system according to which the game is played. Thus, it is similar to the general state of trust which forms the basis for all action in the reality of everyday life (cf. Juchem 1988: 113; Wulff 1994).

Each show situation is constituted twice: with regard to the presentation of the show and of everyday life, and for the participants in their behavioural roles. The same applies to all the other communicative partners of the show's participants – the spectators at home in front of their screens.

Considered more narrowly, behavioural situations have the character of scenic arrangements. In them, sensory-symbolic and sensory-immediate forms of interaction play a central role and thereby represent the experience of sensory discourse with the world. Scenic stagings of game shows are also emotionally constituted in this manner. They involve the staging of situative relevance which is a part of, and the object of, defining situations. In this manner the breaking, or transgression, of rules which is part of the dramaturgy of many games becomes an opportunity to exercise strategies of management and adaptation. Most important is the way in which participants deal with the situation and surmount the task at hand: a communicative challenge, or even a staged crisis. In doing so, they can generally rely upon the rules and norms present in the show situation. The visualization of such processes corresponds to the images of unconscious praxis figures which can only be communicated via sensory-symbolic and sensory-immediate forms of interaction. This is a form of connection of the television texts to the context of the spectator's lifeworld.

> Aesthetic stagings of the life-world as a game recount in concrete physical figures which are able to be staged and experienced, the *drama* of past, hidden and possible life models. The narrative background modulates itself in practical everyday perspective even more strongly towards the direction of a livable drama. Here, life scenes are symbolized in presentative terms as a displayed corporal-scenic narrative of images in dramatized everyday interactions. (Belgrad 1992: 262)

Spectators can recognize their own stories amongst others which are strange to them in the scenic arrangements of television texts during reception (see also Mikos 1994b).

Almost all behavioural roles in television texts, as well as in television productions (shows, news programmes, etc.) and fictional programme forms (television movies, series, etc.) correspond to the structural and functional determination of everyday behavioural roles. This renders them functional for parasocial interaction. The roles in *Wheel of Fortune* are quite clear: host, assistant, an off-screen speaker, three players and an (albeit mostly invisible) studio audience.

- The host focuses all interaction with the players on himself. Furthermore, he structures the situation, provides cue-words and instructions. He embodies power over and control of the situation.
- The assistant turns over on the playing board the letters which have been guessed and presents special prizes and jackpots.
- The off-screen speaker presents the products which have been purchased, as well as sample prizes, special prizes and jackpots.
- The studio audience is only present in the opening establishing shot and remains only audible, not visible, for the rest of the programme. The audience space is hermetically sealed off from what is going on on-stage and what is shown on-screen.

Functional roles in media – specific to television, for example, host, assistants, players – and social behavioural roles are of particular importance for situative game-show analysis. These roles are partly limited to their intended function. The people who carry them out are left with little room to manoeuvre and transform 'role-taking' into 'role-making'. Thus, while the assistant in *Wheel of Fortune* can turn the correctly guessed letters over on the playing board, she remains mute and confined to this role. She only appears in a situation set up for communication when she stands together with the host and the players during the final sequence of the show.

The role of the host permits a relatively greater amount of freedom in role-making. He must explain the show to the guests, players and studio audience. The show's host, the guests and the players are defined via their functional roles in the media. They cannot leave them behind, as this would violate the collective definition of situations. However, as they have to be transferred into behavioural roles, they have a relatively large amount of space in which to create these roles.

Cultural context of *Wheel of Fortune*

According to our thesis, shows adapt situations, problems and games from the spectator's everyday life. This is a precondition for being able to understand role conflicts. It is important for the pleasurable participation of the spectator in the home, who can integrate the action into a personal world of experience. It is also a precondition for the ability to estimate the authority a candidate must possess while being exposed to such a situation. The everyday basis upon which the shows are conceived might be: flirting with the opposite sex, as in *Blind Date* (*Herzblatt*), or the display of everyday skills in crazy acts, as in *Wanna Bet?* (*Wetten Dass?*). Everyday knowledge of prices is playfully brought on-stage in *The Price is Right* (*Der Preis ist Heiss*), which involves estimating or guessing the price of products. Everyday guessing situations are the core and basis of *Wheel of Fortune*.

Solving crossword puzzles is a popular and incredibly widespread leisure activity, as indicated by the number of puzzle books which can be bought at any newspaper stand. In addition almost every weekly newspaper has a permanent puzzle section, as do many dailies. This is one form of amusement which crosses all levels of class, education and income. The level of education of the target group is reflected in the structure and difficulty of the puzzle.

In early civilizations puzzles were often associated with magic or religious rituals. Puzzle questions were part of sacrificial rites and their resolution was often a question of life and death. From the Middle Ages onwards they also served as proof of education. Travelling bards gained entry into the court by pretending to be educated and solving a courtly riddle. The bourgeois concept of a puzzle as thought and memory training is still reflected in today's crossword puzzles. Not only do they prove one's level of education, but they are also a favourite means of killing time.

Whoever solves crossword puzzles shows off her or his knowledge. 'General knowledge' is one of the core values of bourgeois educated culture. There were many quiz shows in the early days of television in which players exhibited more or less specialized knowledge and were tested on it by the host. The host thereby assumed a role closer to that of a 'schoolmaster-examiner' (Fiske 1987, 267) than to that of a 'host'. Whoever wants to guess at the names, etc. in *Wheel of Fortune* must be able to draw upon a large body of general knowledge. This includes common proverbs, idiomatic expressions, figures of popular culture, and more. The playful questioning which tests this body of knowledge is not specialized. The game has a monopoly on the authority which, in other shows, often evokes embarrassing examinations. The background of knowledge is global, diffuse and everyday, and is more likely gained through popular media consumption and everyday experience than through school or reading (Fiske 1987, 267). In this respect, access to the game does not depend on previous specialized education, nor does it require exhibiting a grotesquely twisted degree of expert encyclopedic knowledge. The game is thus a deeply democratic one.

Wheel of Fortune does not stand alone, but takes in other everyday games. An immediate predecessor is 'Hangman' – 'a word game in which one player selects one word which the other player must guess by supplying each of its letters; for each incorrect guess a part of a stick figure of a hanged man is drawn' (Webster's Dictionary). The crossword puzzles mentioned above, as well as the famous games 'Mastermind' and 'Trivial Pursuit', belong to a family of guessing games out of which *Wheel of Fortune* was developed.

The intertextual path which leads from television shows to

generically related games indicates that it is the games which activate the everyday environment of play. Thus the game show stands
in a familiar circle of activity. Crossword puzzles are not solved by
individuals, but form the centre of social activities.

The experience of familiarity and intimacy in such games
invites individual participation. When watching *Wheel of Fortune* on
television one tries out additions to the still empty letter panels on
one's own and formulates hypotheses regarding the likelihood that
a particular letter will appear (and comments on the outcome and
on the differing choices of the studio players). One moves within
the encyclopedic body of knowledge which gives rise to each
maxim or name, and goes back over one's own global knowledge.
This parallel game can be played alone or together with others.[1]

There are further intertextual traces to be found in everyday
situations. The off-screen speaker's voice evokes in tone as well as in
function that of street vendors still familiar on the German high
street, outside department stores and in markets, selling gadgets.
He describes the products, their brand names and prices in a boast-
ful tone which accentuates their supposedly extraordinary quality.[2]

'Extolling'; insisting on the high value of an object; praising its
merits; an eternal chain of compliments: these refer to a social relationship of exchange which casts the exchange itself as an
understanding with reference to the value of the product. It does
not reduce the ritual of this interaction to the scrutiny of price tags.
Selling through praise is part of the interaction of exchange. It finds
its place in the game show by virtue of its mixture of indecency,
volume and direction to a diffuse audience – just as it does at a fairground. In this context it isn't taken seriously and is not a functional
part of a trading transaction. Rather it is a style of presentation of
objects.

It is interesting to note that when a similar technique is
employed in *Wheel of Fortune* it affects the mode of the whole show.
When the game's winnings are spoken of in this manner, they are
assigned status as goods or objects which are not only of value but
also represent 'value' as opposed to pure profit. Whoever takes part
in the game does not only win but also profits from material added
value. The market-crier tone is exactly in keeping with this two-
sided point of view. The objects assume a major role in the overall
game, as if part of a continuous advertising campaign.

At the same time, there is continual reference to the everyday conditions associated with the possession or acquisition of such products. The products which can be won in *Wheel of Fortune* provide information about the everyday consumption and living habits of the players. Products are part of stylistic everyday behaviour. The consumption or possession of objects is part of self-presentation and self-image. One has to be able to relate to the series of objects to be won, or there would be no point in taking part in the game. A constant appeal to the viewer's sociocultural class affiliation is carried out through the selection of winnings alone.[3]

The market-crier quality of the voice-overs corresponds to the iconographic tradition of which *Wheel of Fortune* is recognizably a part. This is, above all, a means of staging something similar to a fairground raffle and employing the patterns of display of a department-store catalogue to present both the game and the products. The arrangement of the products in tableaux, their placement on raffle prize tables, their framing in glittery shop-window frames, and the occasional production of vignette-like images refer back to the culture of product displays. The product is staged as an object which is worth being displayed figuratively. It should be noted that the products are not shown in the manner of a television commercial – the commercials themselves are always set in contrast to the presentation of products during the game and take up almost 20 per cent of the broadcasting time (see Wiedemann 1993: 133).

The products are the hidden stars of *Wheel of Fortune*. One of the major recurring segments of the show involves 'shopping'. Incidentally, this segment is staged identically in all of the different national versions of the show. The face of the winner is faded in as the main image, while the camera pans over the objects on display. A voice-over follows the actual shopping which describes the selected objects (shown again on-screen). This segment takes up almost 30 per cent of the show-time in the German version. In the Scandinavian version it occupies closer to 20 per cent of the time. In the American original it only takes up 10 per cent of the time (Skovmand 1992: 97ff.). The presentation of the products is part of the assistant's role. In addition to her duties in the game, she is charged with the presentation of special prizes. Fiske localizes quiz shows as being generally 'part of commodity capitalism, and us[ing] many [...] similar cultural strategies. For instance, glamorous models are used to display the prizes and thus associate commodities with sexuality, thereby linking buying with sexual desire and satisfaction' (1987: 272). Thus, a whole field of presentation and semiotic techniques is formed. This is an area of cultural practices within which product communication is carried out and where a show such as *Wheel of Fortune* is localized and referred to intertextually.

Let us return to situative description. It is one of the standard topoi – particularly of the critical literature on game shows such as *Wanna Bet? (Wetten Dass?)* or guessing games like *Wheel of Fortune* – to label them with a simple critical ideological model as 'glorifying the achievement principle'. It is debatable whether one wishes to accept this label, or rather see the shows as a playful means of dealing with the demands presented by everyday competitive situations in which the achievement principle plays a role.

The popularity of shows is based above all on the 'linking of, and reference to, immediate life circumstances and the recipient's conception of values' (Müller 1993: 12). The conditions which are produced along with them are anchored in a social context and among the reference points of the spectator's lifeworld. The question remains whether such shows are pure propaganda for the ethical maxims of working life or if they are presented in a diversified manner.

'Play' and 'achievement' seem to contradict one another. So it seems necessary in examining the aspect of achievement to differentiate the game as an observable act and from the conduct of the game as an independent narrative. Even then, determining the quality of achievement is difficult. Whoever plays a game acts in a goal-orientated fashion. One can determine 'achievement' with reference to the goal, to the execution of the narrative and to the conditions of competition. In this sense, 'achievement' is inherent to all the performing arts. The juggler also displays 'achievement' in working with her or his objects. The question of where achievement can be localized is interesting, as admiration of an achievement depends upon being able to determine its contents. The juggler doesn't even show any particular effort. The moves have become routine for her or him. Still, the supreme ease with which he or she masters his or her craft amazes the spectator.

This ease during task-solving is present in *Wheel of Fortune* as well. One can play smart tactically by means of the imaginary purchase of vowels. The early purchase of a vowel may help the other players arrive at the solution. However, to make no purchase is to risk being last to work out the answer. While the players have opportunities to act strategically, applying competitive logic, they remain to a great extent at the mercy of chance.

The functional role of the players in *Wheel of Fortune* depends on strategies and tactics acquired in everyday activity (practice) as described by de Certeau (1984). Whoever's turn it is to spin the wheel has to seize this opportunity in order to win. The strategic element is often subordinated to the grabbing of the opportunity. Tactical everyday behaviour is played off against possible strategies.

Achievement is rewarded in competitive situations. One person is the winner; the other is the loser. The fact that not only a symbolic but also a concrete material profit is gained in game shows plays a part as well. This element is so important in some shows that it can be considered as the real motivation for participating in the game. In this case, the game is primarily defined as a trade relationship.

Participation is the investment on which the players hope to obtain a material return. As participation remains risky, the 'trade' is carried out with the characteristics of a 'wager' or that of a 'joint venture'. The degree of importance for the candidate of a low amount of material gain (relative to everyday income levels) is shown when – as in *Money or Love* (*Geld oder Liebe*) – they can choose at the end whether they want to have the money paid out to them or wish to compete for a symbolic grand prize. The difference between the playful course of the game and the prize money at the end is particularly tangible here.

Even if the game is removed from everyday life, the outcome reverts back to aspects of everyday values. Shows supposedly form their own 'game' reality while remaining rooted in everyday life. They remove themselves from everyday constraints yet still manage to remain close to them. The 'social space' which is unfolded in the shows is also due to the fact that shows adapt principles culled from their audience's everyday work and leisure experiences.

Discursive strategies of game shows

The intertextual arena in which *Wheel of Fortune* is located refers not only to everyday situations and ideological patterns of interpreta-tion but also to cultural history in general and especially to the genre of television entertainment. The cultural background even makes itself felt in the choice of name for the show. The 'wheel of fortune' is an allegorical representation of the alternation of human luck, and human fate and is one of the attributes of Fortuna, the Roman goddess of luck.

Aspects of motivational history of the example being considered here should not interest us at this time. Rather we should focus more narrowly on the intertextual field of television entertainment. *Wheel of Fortune* is a game show. This by itself is problematic, as the borders between the individual subgenres cannot be drawn sharply, and the different subtypes permeate and overlap each other. The development of show-genres can best be summed up as a process of continual miscegenation of forms.

Formal differentiation amongst what are now numerous shows is difficult. Hallenberger (1988) attempted to differentiate the shows according to the type of game, although in doing so he merely used categories with regard to content. Even a distinction between quiz shows and so-called game shows appears problematic, as a quiz can be seen as a guessing game. The apodictic phrase 'Each show is different' (Mikos and Wulff 1989: 61) is fundamentally sound. Game shows exhibit some common formal and integral characteristics despite their multiplicity of forms.

Television programmes where guests and players play games according to predetermined rules under the direction of a host or master of ceremonies can be considered to belong to the game-show genre. Above all, these games involve the playful treatment of everyday situations. Individual subgenres can be formed according to the type of game, for example competitive games like *Family Feud* (*Familienduell*) or *The Honeymoon Show* (*Flitterabend*), guessing or quiz shows such as *The Big Prize* (*Der Grosse Preis*), prize games such as *Wheel of Fortune* (*Glücksrad*) or *Let's Make a Deal* (*Geh Auf's Ganze*), as well as interactive games such as *Money or Love* (*Geld oder Liebe*), *Forgive Me* (*Verzeih Mir*) or *Blind Date* (*Herzblatt*).

The idea of using categories of situativity to analyse the shows is a helpful one. Each individual show presents a framework of situations. Individual episodes are embedded in the overall situation. Each represents situations for itself, and these are then organized into sub-episodes. In this way, a round of the game can be seen as one episode in the show: an independent situation all the same. This situation is organized into sub-episodes, for example a short conversation by the host with the players, the host's introduction to the game, execution of the game, evaluation of the game and possibly a concluding conversation about the game. The segmental organization of interaction during the show is not a matter which is specific to the show; it is part of the communicative organization of everyday life.

Each communication can be organized into phases (these, in turn, being linked by transitional pieces). The more institutionalized a situation is, and/or the more power is assigned to a 'leading figure', the more clearly the individual segments stand next to one another. The transition from one segment to another is much harder to follow in a classroom lesson than it is around a table in a bar. The communicative and institutional power befitting a host manifests itself in his right to introduce a break off individual phases of the show, to carry out the transition from one segment to the next, etc. Show-communication reveals itself to be a highly institutionalized form of communication.

Of course, elements and techniques are present in the shows which provide them with suprasegmental cohesion. There are so-called bridge elements in almost every show: connected episodes which fall into several phases and may bridge several episodes. The 'studio wager' in the show *Wanna Bet? (Wetten Dass?)* has a bridge function. It is introduced at the beginning of the show and spans it until the end. The solution to the 'studio wager' ends the show.

Another example of suprasegmental structure is the fact that the order of numerous competitive shows follows that of a tournament: individual players or pairs of players are eliminated in the individual rounds of the game until a winner remains. The winner must often prove her or his winner's status again in a final game.

What happens in the show itself is introduced, as in news shows or talk shows, by the host. The host's entrance at the beginning of the show is heavily ritualized. Generally, a door opens through which the host enters in order to walk down a couple of steps to reach the level of the audience. The moderator enters from a kind of void into the show's arena of action: the showroom (visible both to the studio audience and to the viewers at home) in which the events of the next hours and minutes will take place. Once the moderator has entered the show-space and placed himself on one level with the audience, he launches into his opening jokes, which bind the spectator more closely to the on-stage action. The moderator presents himself to the audience as a good host who, at least for the time being, wants to put everyone in a good mood so that the 'show/party' can succeed. It is significant to note that at that moment the total show situation is constituted as an essentially social, interactive relationship between the host, the studio audience and the spectators at home.

The host offers the possibility of a relationship with his opening gags which can either be accepted or rejected. He constitutes the show situation as an interactive relationship between himself and the spectators. This is possible because the subsequent order of the show is defined as a show situation in which everyone from the host to the theatre or studio audience to the viewers at home is involved on an interactive and communicative basis. The involvement of the spectators does not occur by their being directly addressed by the host – who also ends the show by bidding farewell to the spectators – but through what happens on-stage. The activity on the show's stage corresponds to the spectator's everyday situations and to their associated behavioural roles.

Opportunities for identification are made and areas for projection are formed via the constellation of behavioural roles. The interactive relationships of the figures involved in the on-stage action create opportunities for transference which result to a great extent from the candidates' role conflicts. The players must act with reference to various elements during the show: to the host, to the other players, to the studio audience in general, to the friends, relatives and acquaintances who might be in the audience as well as to those who might be watching at home, and to the spectator in general. Shows are scenic arrangements in which numerous role conflicts arise from a rich weave of interactive relationships. These, in turn, refer back to everyday situations.

Conclusion

The shows' playing situations refer to the participants' and spectators' everyday experience and their everyday structures of interaction. In their communicative behaviour they activate knowledge regarding conventions of the television-show genre, of game playing outside of the shows, as well as general knowledge about the world in all those concerned – including the viewer in front of the television screen. The show stands in an *intersituative relationship* to everyday life. Those involved must activate *intertextual references* in a show's episodes on two levels: they must refer to appropriate situations in everyday life and to the conventions of the shows.

This applies to the television viewer as well. In order to accept the show's offer of interaction and build parasocial relationships to the persons being shown the spectator must actualize everyday experience as much as experience with the genre in the reception situation. Popular game shows such as *Wheel of Fortune* are forms of cultural praxis on the one hand. On the other they are rooted through the intersituative relationship to the participants' and spectators' reality of everyday life in their social contexts and lifeworld.

Postscript

The description of situative frameworks as well as intersituational and intertextual relationships is one of the tasks of the text theories of television shows. The field of intertextual relationships encompasses three different types of reference. Some relationships are based on, or are found in, the formal characteristics and elements of the texts themselves. Others can be found in the ecological relationship of media consumers and the medium. Finally, a third type are ideological relationships which refer texts, and indeed entire genres, back to deeply seated ideological beliefs.

Notes

1   According to Caviola *et al.* (1992: 54), 69 per cent of all spectators frequently or always guess along with the show; if several people watch the show together, then three quarters guess along; more than 40 per cent of those surveyed stated that they have considered actual participation in the game.

2   Dieter Wiedemann (1993: 133) also refers to the connection to fairground barkers.

3   In addition to the US production, *Wheel of Fortune* is produced in eight European countries (Skovmand 1992: 90). The different national versions frequently differ quite dramatically from one another; only the centrepiece – wheel and letter board – remain unchanged. There is also a computer game of the same name. In the USA, where it originated in 1975, *Wheel of Fortune* lasts sixty minutes and attracts 40 million viewers. The German version, *Glücksrad*, began in 1988 with half-hour shows, moving on to forty-five-minute shows in 1990. The Danish version, *Lykkehjulet*, is broadcast in Denmark on TV2, the second Danish channel, and throughout Scandinavia via satellite on TV3. Little is known about the *Glücksrad* audience. 58.3 per cent of viewers are 50 years old and over (Pretsch 1991: 731; see also Caviola *et al.* 1992: 49). Skovmand (1992: 91) describes the US audience as diverse, with a definite tendency towards the lower middle class, 'with a bias

towards the demographically interesting target group of women between 25 and 54'. Caviola *et al.* (1992: 50ff.) describe similar tendencies amongst the German audience.

References

Belgrad, Jürgen (1992), *Identität als Spiel. Eine Kritik des Indentätskonzepts von Jürgen Habermas*, Opladen: Westdeutscher Verlag.

Caviola, Sandra, Drazic, Vera, Schulz, Petra, Krobb, Marion (1992), *Von Waren und Weibern. Eine Analyse der Werbegameshows 'Glücksrad' und 'Der Preis ist Heiss' und ihres Publikums*, MS, Münster.

de Certeau, Michel (1984), *The Practice of Everyday Life*, Berkeley: University of California Press.

Fiske, John (1987) *Television Culture*, London: Methuen.

Hallenberger, Gerd (1988), 'Fernseh-Spiele. Über den Wert und Unwert von Game-shows und Quizsendungen', *TheaterZeitSchrift* 26: 17–28.

Habermas, Jürgen (1988), *Theorie des kommunikativen Handelns*, vol. 2, Frankfurt: Suhrkamp.

Hügel, Hans-Otto and Müller, Eggo (eds) (1993), *Fernsehshows: Form- und Rezeptionsanalyse*, Hildesheim: Universität Hildesheim (Medien und Theater 1).

Juchem, Johann G. (1988), *Kommunikation und Vertrauen. Ein Beitrag zum Problem der Reflexität in der Ethnomethodologie*, Aachen: Alano.

Mikos, Lothar (1994a), *Fernsehen im Erleben der Zuschauer. Vom lustvollen Umgang mit einem populären Medium*, Berlin and Munich: Quintessenz.

—— (1994b), 'Perceiving reality as fiction. Television narratives as formations of fantasies', *Interface* 6: 153–63.

—— and Wulff, Hans J. (1989), 'Zur Analyse von Unterhaltungsshows. 1. Höhepunkte des Fernsehalltags', *Medien praktisch* 13.4: 60–2.

Müller, Eggo (1993), *Ausstellung der (Selbst-) Darstellung von geschlechtsrollenbildern. Zur fernsehanalytische Strategie John Fiskes am Beispiel 'Herzblatt'*, MS, Berlin.

Skovmand, Michael (1992), 'Barbarous TV International: Syndicated "Wheels of Fortune"'. *Media Cultures. Reappraising transnational media*, ed. Michael Skovmand and Kim Christian Schroder, London: Routledge (Communication and Society), 84–103.

Wiedemann, Dieter (1993), 'Mentales Teleshopping', in Hügel and Müller (eds) (1993), 131–4.

Wulff, Hans-Jürgen (1993), 'Situationalität. Vorbemerkungen zur Analyse von "Glücksrad" – Exemplaren', in Hügel and Müller (eds) (1993), 120–4.

—— (1994), 'Situationalität, Spieltheorie, kommunikative Konstellation: Bemerkungen zur pragmatischen Fernseh-Analyse', in *Aspekte der Fernsehanalyse. Methoden und Modelle*. Ed. Knut Hickethier, Münster/Hamburg: Lit Verlag (Beiträge zur Medienästhetik und Mediengeschichte 1).

7

Creator Spiritus: virtual texts in everyday life

BEN BACHMAIR

Media reception as poiesis

A 10-year-old German boy was asked about his favourite film, and recounted the story of Eddie Murphy's comedy *The Distinguished Gentleman*. He kept close to the general outline of this story of an honourable little crook, and mentioned key episodes in the film. However, his main focus was on themes that were of special importance to him, namely those of illness and of the alarming degradation of a child. The image of the child in danger seemed to him to represent his own immediate emotional state, because he had recently had to move house and reorientate himself in unfamiliar and difficult social surroundings.

A glance around the same boy's bedroom revealed posters of pop stars, a TV listings magazine, several videos, clothes in the 'rocker' style then fashionable among German children, and a Nintendo Gameboy. Media texts, from favourite films to TV advertisements for clothes, are a fundamental part of the world which a child assembles for itself into an integrated whole. However simple it may appear, this unifying process now forms a historically and culturally specific relation between individuals and the media, in which meanings are established by individuals' incorporating diverse symbolic resources into 'texts' personal to them.

In the sense that they are not available for inspection in material form, these texts are virtual in nature, but they can be read off through such symbolic performances as conversations, a quotation chosen from a film, or a choice of furniture. Their unity is a stylistic one based on the symbolic resources found in everyday life and incorporated into them, including products such as clothes and furniture as well as those transmitted by the media (films, videos, computer games and books). Thus in summarizing *The Distinguished Gentleman*, the boy was showing the ability to do two distinct things: because he had incorporated his experience of the film into the stylistically unified pattern of his life, he was able to use his summary as a means of expressing something about himself.

This process can be understood by reference to a pair of theoretical concepts: mimesis and poiesis. With the help of these concepts we can classify the various possible relationships between individuals and the media according to the historical and cultural contexts in which they have actually existed (see Gebauer and Wulff 1992). In present-day consumer-orientated industrial societies, the relationship between individuals and the media is not primarily one where the audience responds to media texts in a manner prescribed by the texts themselves. This type of reproduction and repetition of textual meaning is what is meant here by the term mimesis. Today, however, individuals mould the symbolic material of their cultural environment into the virtual texts of their own everyday lives (Schütz 1962). These virtual texts then find objective expression in symbolic performances such as fitting out a child's bedroom (Gerlach 1993: 30–4). This type of functional displacement, involving the active production of meaning, is what is meant here by the term poiesis.

Reception as mimesis and as poiesis: from Goethe's *Werther* to the virtual text

It is superficially true that media texts reflect something else, but this is no longer their primary function, which is rather to provide symbolic resources for incorporation into the virtual texts of everyday life. The decisive process of producing meanings does not therefore take place in the studio, but when individuals select and incorporate into these virtual texts those elements provided by the media which they find most useful. The relationship between the media and their audiences is therefore now a hermeneutic one. What this means is that the part played by the audience in the production of meaning is no less important than that played by the reports, stories and so forth transmitted by the media themselves.

In Germany, the origins of this hermeneutic relationship between the media and their audiences can be found in the eighteenth-century *Sturm und Drang* movement, and certain passages of Goethe's novel *The Sorrows of Young Werther* are particularly important in this respect. The *Sturm und Drang* reacted subversively against the social constraints and traditional literary models of the feudal state and society, stressing instead the creative power of individual imagination, and the value of subjective experience (Schmidt 1988: 35 and 47; Jorgensen *et al.* 1990: 425). Rather than attempting to reiterate mimetically some set of supposedly objective events in the external world, these writers viewed themselves as casting an inner world of emotion and imagination in a literary form that made it communicable. Thus the meditations of Goethe's character Werther link mimesis *vis-à-vis* the external world with social constraint, and contrast both with creative poiesis.

Yet because reading, unlike writing, was not considered to be an autonomous creative process, the audience mimetically repeated the experiences and viewpoints expressed by the author in the text, to the point of experiencing similar emotions. This is, for example, the reason why contemporary critics thought it inevitable that readers of Goethe's *Werther* would follow the novel's hero in committing suicide. More generally, mimetic realization of the supposed individuality of the writers of the *Sturm und Drang* played a part in shaping the development of new and specifically bourgeois (post-feudal) ways of life, for example among those of their readers who were brought together of their own free will in circles animated by these interests. Thus the *Sturm und Drang* articulated a conception of human nature according to which subjectivity was formed by individuals shaping their own lives in reaction to their experiences. This conception of poiesis gained ground at the time of the French Revolution (Schütz 1962), before becoming a general model for modern societies.

As the model suggests, human beings in the industrial and consumer societies of the present day are the unique creators of the virtual texts of their own everyday lives. This has been made increasingly clear by the development of the media away from public-service broadcasting modelled on the BBC's policy of balanced and responsible programming. By implication at least, this type of broadcasting required of its audience a mimetic response. It has now been largely superseded, and popular demand has played a part in this: it is no longer widely considered to provide the virtual texts of individuals' everyday lives with adequate symbolic resources. It has therefore everywhere been more or less completely replaced by the market model, where individual viewers compile their own schedules on a self-service basis from a 'buffet' of symbolic resources. Viewing figures regulate what the buffet puts on offer. Selection from the buffet and integration of what has been selected into the virtual text of everyday life is an individualized process, and it is here that meanings are produced. There is already a body of literature on the functional rules of such processes (see Charlton and Bachmair (eds) 1990, Fiske 1993, Silverstone 1994, Bachmair 1996).

The production of meanings in this manner is characteristic of societies dominated by the media and by consumption. Such societies' individualized social and cultural activities presuppose that people bestow personal meanings on media texts and other symbolic resources, shaping the virtual texts of their own everyday lives on the basis of all such resources as they choose to pursue at any given time. Of course, people living in industrial societies before the development of television were also engaged in similar processes, but these were much more restricted in their range and variety because the symbolic resources available were less varied. In recent times the media have progressively penetrated more and more areas of existence, and, through advertising, have become very closely associated with the provision of goods and services as well. When they are considered in all their variants from films to MTV, television pictures may be seen to have become interwoven with so many areas of experience as themselves to be the basic building blocks of the virtual texts of individuals' everyday lives in today's 'reflexive risk society' (Beck 1986). The uses to which people put this symbolic material need to be understood from at least three different perspectives all at the same time: (1) in the context of their own lives and personal interests; (2) relative to their existing or desired social environment; (3) within the framework of the media in general.

The following case studies illustrate this phenomenon.

The film *E.T.* told backwards

Some boys in the same primary-school class were heard talking about the difficulties one of them was having with his swimming, and with his swimming equipment. Initially, the exchange between

Sven and Markus in particular seemed limited, undeveloped, and chaotic.

> Teacher: So that you have everything you need, I want you to bring your swimming things tomorrow, your soap, and your money.
> Boy: Yes, yes.
> Teacher: Remember your goggles as well.
> Sven: No, I'm not bringing goggles. I've had enough. I've hurt myself enough. I've hurt myself enough. I'm not doing it any more. I've done it once and I'm not doing it any more.

Sven reacted strongly against the usually unproblematic suggestion that the children bring their swimming gear with them to school. What did he mean by 'hurting' himself? Clearly he was making a connection between his swimming equipment and unpleasant experiences, but what did he mean by this?

Sven was a child who had had severe and repeated illnesses, and had been to hospital many times. This had meant that he was often unable to do his homework. He also came from a home where he received no help with his homework, and where there was no money for swimming equipment. This was the old hurt that Sven did not want to face again.

Dieter did not understand this, so Sven had to rationalize and clarify his argument about hurting himself by claiming to have an allergy.

> Dieter: Really? Why not?
> Sven: It's so bad ... I'm allergic to goggles ...
> Markus: Yeah! And I bet the teacher'll buy that!
> Sven: I do get an allergy! Everything gets sore and it really hurts ...
> Dieter: Hmm ... he's telling the truth about that ...

The topic of the children's conversation was by this stage the question whether the teacher would believe in Sven's 'allergy'. Now that Sven's references to his illness had to some degree persuaded Dieter of the gravity of his difficulties with swimming, he changed tack somewhat, showing himself as he did so to be somewhat insecure in his image of himself.

> Sven: Of course, I know I'm not a human being.
> Teacher: So what are you then?

The teacher was too busy with more commonplace matters to give her full attention to a claim so potentially disruptive as Sven's second one, that he was not human. In an attempt to make himself understood, Sven himself now introduced a new term, Autorifon, whose significance in fact appeared to be grasped only by Markus.

> Sven: I'm an Autorifon ... oh yes, I've been to hospital ...
> Markus: Like E.T. .... is that his right name?...
> Sven: E.T.
> *(Reassuring Markus that he was right.)*
> Markus: ... when he gets ill ...

Sven, and now Markus too, were referring to an episode from the film *E.T.*, about a clever, sensitive being from outer space, roughly the same size as a child and with a body and features similar to human ones, but also liable to be taken for an animal. They went on to develop their shared understanding of the episode's relevance, and of the life-threatening dangers faced by E.T. in the film.

> Sven: Yes. He's all white. It's because he's homesick, that's why ...
> and when he lay in the water ...
> Markus: *(squeal)*

Sven was stressing how close E.T. comes in the film to death, which is the meaning of his turning 'all white', and linking this both to homesickness and to another episode where E.T., 'in the water', is again in life-threatening danger. But he soon changed tack again, referring to a third episode: to their mutual terror the alien E.T. is discovered by the young boy Elliot, and in the absence of any common language they begin to communicate by sharing sweets. This is the beginning of their friendship.

> Sven: E.T., but ... when he sat in the grass and then he said ... and
> then him there ... he did that ... *(following by squeals)*
> Markus: I think it's good ... at the beginning ... when he sort of ...
> with the Smarties ... ha! ha! *(followed by laughter, and smacking of
> the lips as though he were eating)*.

Comparison with the film shows that the children's quotations from it did not follow the order in which they appear in the story, but were selected on thematic grounds. Their association of E.T. with the idea of hospital brings into the foreground a central episode of the film where adults' lack of understanding endangers the life of the extraterrestrial E.T., who must therefore die. Only the little boy Elliot's love brings E.T. back to life. In the film, the children and E.T. together escape from the rigid, inflexible adults' world on mountain bikes, but rather than recall this, Sven and Markus worked backwards towards the beginning of the story, where E.T. and Elliot overcome their initial fear and horror by sharing Smarties.

By focusing their conversation on this part of the story, Sven and Markus were able to thematize something that they were themselves doing: tentatively and gradually forming a friendship in an otherwise hostile or indifferent world. Neither Dieter nor the teacher was able to relate the film fragments to this thematic context, and they were therefore unable to follow the conversation beyond a certain point: Sven and Markus had formed or discovered a social bond from which Dieter and the teacher were excluded. They had done this by sharing in a process of poiesis which, because they shared in it in this way, could be observed.

TV genre in social space

A group of children were observed in a school playground, taking turns to perform a dance to their favourite song. The basic framework for these performances was copied from the format of the German RTL television series *Mini Playback Show*, a very popular programme sometimes watched by over 60 per cent of German children aged 6–13. As in the television programme, individual children or groups of two to three followed each other in standing on a small staircase in front of the peer group and dancing to a song by their favourite group or star, whose clothes and choreography they also copied to the degree that they were able. Where the children's performances in the playground differed from those seen on television was in being based on the current hit parade rather than on a repertoire of golden oldies.

The popularity of the television programme meant that shared knowledge of its format provided the group with a common point of reference despite the children's preferences for various different styles of music. Thus the children were able to use a shared activity and common knowledge of the media as a means of mapping out the differences between their preferred styles without becoming involved in heated discussion or argument. The result was a tacit understanding, based on complex combinations of sounds and images and held in common by the whole group, of differences within it.

Listed below are five examples of the children's performances in the playground:

Guns 'n' Roses – 'Don't damn me'

Guns 'n' Roses play hard rock. Their image evokes that of the Rolling Stones, and themes of sex, drugs and rock 'n' roll are prominent.

One boy wore a T-shirt with a picture of the group's leader Axl Rose, and all of the boys imitated the band in wearing headbands which also evoke the character of the lone fighter Rambo. The song they performed had at that time been released on CD only; in the absence of a video they had had to devise and agree their own choreography.

Nicki – 'Ich bin a bayrisches Cowgirl' ('I'm a Bavarian cowgirl')

In complete contrast to Guns 'n' Roses, Nicki mixes elements of country, pop and traditional German folk styles. Her image is that of a friendly, conformist girl from a nice family, who left her business apprenticeship at the age of 16 to become a successful singer.

The girl imitating her in the school playground likewise presented an appearance of wholesomeness, honesty and proper upbringing. She performed silently, miming the words of the German song in time with the recording.

Boyz II Men – 'All 4 love'

Boyz II Men are four black youths who perform a 'soft' rap.

This song, which had been released on video, was performed by two girls wearing black shoes and trousers, T-shirts under colourful shirts, and baseball caps. Their performance was sufficiently co-ordinated to show that they had rehearsed with care.

Die Prinzen (The Princes) – 'Ich war so gerne Millionär' ('I wish I were a millionaire')

The Princes were an East German band who moved to the West after the reunification of Germany. The five members of the band wear jeans, denim jackets and striking T-shirts. They cultivate a laid-back image and favour casual chat when interviewed.

In the school playground, a single girl danced to the song, performing alone but in careful imitation of the group's style. She had not agreed with other children beforehand on a favourite group and choreography, but the group and the song are well known from a video as well as a CD, and her performance was well received.

Michael Jackson – 'Why you wanna trip me'

Michael Jackson is not easy to imitate as he has his own distinctive style of performance which requires advanced dancing skills. The difficulty was increased in this case because no video of this song had been released.

A girl dressed in Michael Jackson-style clothes followed his complicated example in every detail of her performance. She must have developed a generic Jackson dance routine, and had probably practised very hard. Her perfect rendition of a well-known song filled the children watching with enthusiasm.

However commonplace these accounts may appear, the performances in the playground involved a complex social interaction between the children. Their own presentations enabled them to distinguish themselves from the peer group and integrate themselves into it at the same time. The high degree of co-operation between them enabled them to fit very diverse styles and preferences into a common framework, thus combining individuality with mutuality: each child's musical preferences and favoured lifestyle were compared with the different ones of other children before then being accepted as part of the general pattern of the programme as it was re-enacted by the group. What made this possible was the format of the popular television programme, which the children had integrated into the virtual text of their shared social space.

Fred's world

During his early twenties, Fred attended a youth centre where he spent several days painting a picture of several nuclear power stations with lava flowing from them. When his picture was finished, he discussed it with a social worker, explaining it partly by reference to details from two films, *The China Syndrome* and *Solent Green*.

The China Syndrome is a political thriller in which a journalist uncovers the corruption that has led to an accident in a nuclear reactor. As a result, the head engineer loses his faith in technology and wages a war against deception for which he is shot as a psychopath by power-station employees. The science-fiction film *Solent Green* is concerned with the inhumanity of life in the aftermath of a nuclear disaster. A policeman discovers that an old friend of his who died in a euthanasia clinic was in fact killed to be used for food: society as a whole has turned or been turned cannibalistic. In the central character Thorn's words, 'They're making our food from human flesh. It won't be long before they start breeding people for food, like cattle'.

In explaining his picture to the social worker, Fred also referred to alarming events from which he seemed to feel insufficiently distanced. These included the nuclear accident at Chernobyl, which had happened the year before, and traumatic scenes from his own childhood, including violent arguments between his parents. While devising the theme of his picture and then painting it, Fred had had time to think about these events, and to set them in a perspective that then enabled him to talk about them. At several different stages in the discussion, it was apparent that Fred was drawing the symbolic resources necessary for this purpose from the films. For instance, he combined quotations and references to *The China Syndrome* with details of the Chernobyl accident. Together these enabled him to construct an explanation of nuclear catastrophe that included elements both of technical error and of the kind of moral and political irresponsibility he believed liable to cause such errors. Fred outlined the normal functioning and the catastrophic technical disfunctioning of the nuclear reactor: 'If the rods are really hot ... there's water all around them and then they'll be cooled down at any rate ... and exactly what happened at Chernobyl happened here ... there was no more cooling ... the whole reactor normally explodes'. He then followed in minute detail the film's account of the course of events leading to disaster, moving from technical matters to the broader context of irresponsible profit-seeking, manipulation and complicity. He highlighted this by contrasting it with the dangerous struggle of a few brave men and women against it.

Fred also inserted central episodes from the science-fiction film *Solent Green* into his account of nuclear catastrophe. These included one where people at a hunger demonstration are crushed beneath a steamroller, and one where an old man about to die in a euthanasia clinic is allowed to watch a film about nature in an intact and harmonious state. Reference to these episodes enabled Fred to develop his interest in depicting inhuman oppression following in the wake of catastrophe and in the salvaging of hope from memories of a harmonious past that preceded it:

> Then I just wanted to show what it was like before. What the world was like before. There are a lot of films where it shows ... uh ... destroyed ... nuclear war ... the people live on, but none of them show what it was like before. Oh, except in one single film. There's no more oxygen, no life, there's only these ... these cells. And the people ... there's only green bread to eat. And that's human flesh. And ... one guy says, right at the end, 'I want to go to sleep and never wake up'. At the end, they can choose exactly what they want to see. And this guy, he'd never seen the world, not like we see it now – a buzzard in the sky, an eagle, and the fields all normal in the spring and summer. But they only know this background ... only grey. Grey on grey. Big dredgers ... they flattened everything.
>
> ... demonstration ... with the police ... rubber truncheons and then real steamrollers, that just advanced on the people, over them, shovelled them away and dumped them behind. Then took them to be exterminated or something. And then there's this guy ... it's shown ... he said, 'I can't live in this world any more, I can't stand it any longer', because he knew what the bread was, you see! ... Nobody knew what it was, and he went into it, and he still had a young friend, and he said, 'I can't tell you, if it comes out I'll be killed'. Then at the end his friend is shot in the tent and says, 'Say it now, tell me what it is'. With the last of his strength he shouted it out in the tent, really shouted it out: 'Green bread is human flesh'.

Faced with the horror of the end of humanity, both Fred's films rely on the hope of salvation through the efforts of courageous individuals. This is in keeping with the genre of the political thriller, where heroes bravely oppose the threat posed by unscrupulous exploiters and gangsters. Again in both films, investigations and the discovery of important information play an integral part in the struggle against large-scale deception (and this is what differentiates political thrillers from action movies). In *The China Syndrome* there are two characters responsible for the discovery of this type of information: a courageous young female reporter who is committed to truth and social responsibility, and the head engineer, who exposes corruption but pays for it with his life. In *Solent Green* it is the detective who does not allow himself to be pacified or bought with modest privileges, but instead reveals the truth of society's having fallen into cannibalism.

In addition to these feats of resistance and dedication to the truth on the part of heroic individuals, both films also feature a father-figure who sacrifices himself. Fred, however, made no reference to the misunderstood head engineer of *The China Syndrome*, but tended instead to stick to technical details in his references to that film. On the other hand, and as we have seen above, his references to *Solent Green* placed the scene of the old man's death in the foreground. In this scene, the good old days of the past are shown in a utopian light. This effect is created by the film that the old man is allowed to watch shortly before his death, which shows an unviolated nature, including animals in beautiful countryside, and is accompanied by a soundtrack of classical music taken from symphonies by Beethoven and Tchaikovsky.

The associated images of utopia and of the father-figure who sacrifices himself are in direct contrast to Fred's own past and present experience: his upbringing had been marked by his father's threatening and aggressive behaviour towards his mother, and he still appeared to view himself as living in a fragile and endangered world. By using symbolic resources drawn from the films he had seen, he was able to express these feelings and experiences, and talk to the social worker about them.

Poiesis today: lifestyle as the new form of social distinction

When Fred wanted to explain the meaning of his painting, he made reference to sequences from different films, which he combined with each other in a complex pattern. This showed the complexity of the imaginative process which was going on even before Fred began to verbalize it. However, the capacity of individuals to create meanings is ultimately circumscribed by the limited range of symbolic resources available to them. In this instance, the creative process depended on Fred's being familiar with specific cinematic genres, which also set limits to the range of associative links he was able to make. In this sense, his creativity was still in some degree controlled or restricted by an element of mimesis (in the sense of the term given on pp. 116–18 above). Yet in contemporary society restrictions on this kind appear to be becoming less and less rigid: there is an increasing tendency towards poiesis.

Multimedia computer applications, together with the linkage of these and television to the 'information superhighway', have brought into being communication or information networks which tend to eliminate the distinctions between familiar genres. This makes it possible to combine elements from texts of different genres in an unprecedently flexible way. At the same time, other changes in society are encouraging this. As a broader range of media and information becomes available to more and more people, increasingly individualized patterns of symbolic behaviour are a typical result, and indeed an inevitable one. In this way, lifestyles (and individual choices between them) are becoming ever more important as a form of social differentiation or distinction.

For the sake of comparison, we can look back a generation or so, to the early days of television broadcasting. In the 1950s and 1960s television developed in the context of a hierarchically structured society, stratified according to levels of income, occupational categories and educational qualifications. Culture, of which television was a part, reflected this hierarchical structure, and served as a means of distinguishing between its component strata – high, middle and low. Television audiences could be categorized as belonging to one of these social strata and targeted accordingly with the appropriate types of programme and schedule.

Currently, however, this older type of vertical, hierarchical structure is giving way to a newer, horizontal one that cuts across it and groups together people of different levels of income, occupations and formal educational backgrounds. This is based on stylistic differentiation and on the range of cultural practices (such as leisure pursuits, patterns of media consumption and fashion choices) from which such differentiation emerges. Thus children, young people and even adults differentiate themselves from each other and assert their individuality by means of the types of clothes and fashion accessories which they either buy or reject. These items are just a few among an abundance of other consumer goods, media products and leisure activities that serve similar purposes.

An illustration of what is meant here can be found in the photograph used in a recent advertisement in the regional press for the southern German fashion-clothing chain Nikeshop. In an empty corner of an urban landscape dominated by violet clouds, a black basketball player in sportswear plays against a young white boy in street clothes including a sweatshirt and a baseball cap worn back-to-front. The combination of basketball with the atmosphere and some of the features of an open-air disco (hip-hop, oversized clothing worn with baseball caps and expensive training shoes, consumption of Coke) immediately tells those in the know that what they are doing is playing streetball. However, streetball is not simply a new sport: it is the focus of a youth scene whose image is one of emergence from the ghetto. The process of communication organized around players' bodies is therefore more than just a series of moves in a game: activities, music, clothes and other consumer items are gathered together and labelled as the means of identification with the relevant group. The potential market for these products is therefore clear, and it is correspondingly easy to plan the marketing of clothing, sporting equipment, CDs, and radio and TV stations. In addition to playing its part in this marketing process, advertising provides youth culture with elements of the symbolic framework that organizes it.

A second illustration of the development of a new structure of subcultural styles and social milieux is to be found in an audience survey published in 1994 by the private German television station Pro7 (SINUS 1994). According to this survey, Pro7 viewers cannot be classified in terms of a simple vertical model of social and cultural stratification, since variations in viewing preferences and in their significance in the context of viewers' everyday lifestyles depend on viewers' values as well as their social status. Social status is charted on a five-point scale (lower, lower-middle, middle, upper-middle and upper class), while values are categorized in such a way as to take into account a continuing process of change in society. The 'traditional' aim of maintaining one's social status is ranged with the 'materialistic' aim of maximizing ownership of possessions, the 'hedonistic' aim of pursuing enjoyment, and the 'post-materialist' aim of achieving personal fulfilment. Finally, a fifth 'post-modernist' pattern of aspiration combines the aims of materialism and post-materialism with that of hedonism. Viewers are located on a grid constructed on the basis of these two intersecting classifications, in groups identified by such labels as 'relaxation seekers', 'media surfers', 'emotional viewers' and 'action fans' (SINUS 1994: 13, 30, 47, 64).

'Relaxation seekers' include both men and women. They tend

to have demanding careers and to favour leisure activities that they consider active and eventful means of broadening personal experience while also relieving stress. They aspire to have an influential voice in society, and to be well informed; they are correspondingly disposed to be highly critical and preoccupied with their own image. But there are some sharp contradictions between their pretensions and their behaviour. They do use TV as a source of information, but more often it is a means of relaxation: their stated preference is for feature films, but they also favour, as stress relievers, programmes which they class as 'easy stuff'.

'Media surfers' are relatively young people, for whom television has been a feature of their upbringing. They tend to have a wide circle of friends and enjoy a very wide variety of leisure activities. They adopt an alert and critical stance, but it tends to be one that they defend as being flexible rather than academic or 'blinkered'. They watch TV irregularly but frequently, switching freely and easily between media, TV channels and different types of programme: they will watch anything they find entertaining, favouring feature films and series in particular.

'Emotional viewers' are housewives and mothers whose lives typically revolve around their families. Even their leisure time tends to be spent at home, and they express a need to overcome boredom through emotion and a sense of participation in the life of a broader community. They watch television frequently and regularly, using it almost exclusively as a source of entertainment and regarding it as an essential part of their everyday lives. They favour shows, 'soft' films and family series that satisfy their need to identify emotionally.

'Action fans' tend to be male craftsmen and manual workers who desire a sense of freedom and independence that they pursue in their free time, and cultivate the image of the strong man. They regularly turn to the media for the excitement of strong stimuli and variation, favouring fast-moving programmes of information and entertainment, including in particular action movies and televised sport. They reject programmes that they think are soppy or encourage passivity.

The consumerism of contemporary society clearly plays a major part in the establishment and differentiation of such lifestyles as those listed above. Sport, for example, offers a framework within which a variety of styles and themes are differentiated and dramatized. For instance, wrestling and streetball offer their devotees two contrasting styles. Wrestling is a grotesque and entirely non-verbal bodily enactment of a ritual fight, whereas streetball players negotiate among themselves who plays with whom, where, when and how. The important difference is between the ritual on the one hand and the negotiation on the other: it is a difference between lifestyle preferences rather than between levels in a social or cultural hierarchy.

Besides sport, lifestyle choices available to young people include various types of popular musical and street styles, techno or hip-hop, punk or skinhead (Polhemus 1994). Other comparable but less visible groupings are those of computer hackers or video fans (Eckert *et al.* 1991, Vogelgesang 1991). Thus individuals construct lifestyles for themselves in an independent and creative fashion, using for this purpose a broad range of other consumer goods as well as their preferred patterns of media consumption. These then cease to be independent and isolated elements, beginning instead to act as intertextual, interrelating components of complex thematic arrangements, and crystallizing around nuclei such as those from the German audience survey listed above. In this way, the everyday lifeworlds of such a society become aesthetically and stylistically differentiated as individuals construct their coherent personal lifeworlds from whatever type and variety of symbolic material may be available to them.

References and Bibliography

Bachmair, B. (1996), *Fernsehkultur. Subjektivität in einer Welt bewegter Bilder*, Opladen: Westdeutscher Verlag.

Beck, U. (1986), *Risikogesellschaft. Auf dem Weg in einer andere Moderne*, Frankfurt: Suhrkamp.

Charlton, M. and Bachmair, B. (eds) (1990), *Medienkommunikation im Alltag. Interpretative Studien zum Medienhandeln von Kindern und Jugendlichen*, Munich: Sauer. (*Media Communication in Everyday Life: Interpretative Studies on Children's and Young People's Media Actions.* Communication Research and Broadcasting No. 9, New York: Sauer).

Eckert, R., Vogelgesang, W., Wetzstein, T. A., Winter, R. (1991), *Grauen und Lust – die Inszenierung der Affekte. Eine Studie zum abweichenden Video-konsum*, Pfaffenweiler: Centaurus.

Eckert, R., Vogelgesang, W., Wetzstein, T. A., Winter, R. (1991), *Auf Digitalen Pfaden. Die Kulturen von Hackern, Programmierern, Crackern und Spielern*, Opladen: Westdeutscher Verlag.

Ferchhoff, W. (1993), *Jugend an der Wende des 20. Jahrhunderts. Lebensformen und Lebensstile*, Opladen: Leske and Budrich.

Fiske, J. (1993), *Television Culture*, London: Routledge.

Gebauer, G. and Wulf, C. (1992), *Mimesis. Kultur – Kunst – Gesellschaft*, Reinbek: Rowohlt.

Gerlach, F. (1993), 'Medien im Kinderzimmer. Medienspuren in Zimmern von Mädchen und Jungen', *Medien praktisch* 4.

Goethe, J. W. von (1988), *Die Leiden des jungen Werthers*, 1st edn 1774, 2nd edn 1787, Munich: Beck.

Jorgensen, S., Bohnen, K. and Ohrgaard, P. (1990), *Enlightenment, Sturm und Drang, Early Classics. 1740–1789*, History of German Literature Volume VI: From the Beginnings to the Present, general eds H. de Boor and R. Newald, Munich: Beck.

Müller, H.-P. (1992), *Sozialstruktur und Lebenstile. Der neuere theoretische Diskurs über soziale Ungleichheit*, Frankfurt: Suhrkamp.

Polhemus, Ted (1994), *Street Style, from Sidewalk to Catwalk*, London: Thames & Hudson.

Schmidt, J. (1988), *The History of German Genius. Thought in German Literature, Philosophy and Politics 1750–1945*. Volume 1. *From the Beginnings to Idealism*, 2nd edn, Darmstadt: Wissenschaftliche Buchgesellschaft.

Schütz, A. (1962), *Collected Papers I. the Problem of Social Reality*, ed. and introd. Maurice Natanson, The Hague, Boston and London: Martinus Nijhoff.

Silverstone, R. (1994), *Television and Everyday Life*, London: Routledge.

SINUS Institute of Social Sciences (1994), 'Structural analysis of Pro7 viewers. Results of a qualitatively orientated pilot study', MGM media group, Munich and Heidelberg, May.

Vogelgesang, W. (1991), *Jugendliche Video-Cliquen. Action- und Horrorvideos als Kristallisationspunkte einer neuen Fankultur*, Opladen: Westdeutscher Verlag.

8

Text as the punctuation of semiosis: pulling at some of the threads

GUNTHER KRESS

Looking at text in a social-semiotic framework

This chapter challenges the category of 'intertextuality' by suggesting that it exists in order to patch up a problem caused by starting with the wrong theory in the first place. So the chapter also poses a challenge to notions of what language is and how it works, which underpin, in often very different ways, many contemporary theories of language. My contention is that in a plausible theory of language the need for the category of 'intertextuality' largely disappears; and where it continues to be used, its function is much altered.

To do this some new thinking is called for – not so much to say completely new things as to put insights which have been available in different places, for many years, into a new arrangement. The framework that I use to do this is that of social semiotics (see Halliday 1978, Hodge and Kress 1988). In this approach semiosis as social activity is the starting point, and the text (as complex sign) is the focal unit of language. Social semiotics assumes that when we interact through language (as well as through other modes) in the complexities of our social environments, we produce texts: linguistic objects which reflect in all their aspects the meanings of the social environment and occasion in which they were made. These can be analysed, after the event, as sentences or clauses; but text is focal. We – as language users – have a good sense when a conversation is finished or a lecture, an interview or the news on television is completed. These are textual entities, made in a particular social environment. I need a job; I go to a job interview; I do my best to meet the many questions put to me; I might ask one question at the end; I leave. Not all these environments are so clearly structured; nevertheless we seem not to have problems understanding what they are. While I am engaged in the conversation or the interview, my focus is *not* on producing phrases, clauses or sentences; my focus is on *participating* in the conversation, or in the interview.

These textual units are co-extensive, in their duration, with social occasions. In their form they reflect crucial aspects of those occasions: the fact that as an interviewee it is not my job to put the interviewers at their ease; that it is my job to answer rather than to ask questions, to make my questions fit into the allocated time, to be sensitive to the social environment in which I am acting through language. Texts have shape; and much of that shape comes from such factors. This shape has been referred to, increasingly over the last fifteen years or so, as *genre*. (See Swales 1990, Cope and Kalantzis (eds) 1993.)

In this approach language always occurs as text: as speakers we participate in making texts, and we do so as hearers also. Texts are social – whether as 'text in the making' or text as completed, material object – reflecting the purposes of their makers and the social characteristics of the environments in which they were made. Consequently we always encounter language as text, and we encounter text in generic form.

To put this the other way around, we do not, ever (except in language-learning, in textbooks or in dictionaries) meet language in the form of isolated words, or clauses, or even sentences. We encounter language as generically formed text. Yet a persistent and dominant common sense insists that language is 'made up' of sounds and words, and words and sentences; and that in speaking or writing we proceed in that fashion: building up larger units from smaller units (phonemes to syllables, morphemes to words, words to phrases, etc.). In this 'constituency view' a text is built 'from bottom up': a large entity is assembled from small and successively larger elements. Small grammatical and/or meaningful bits are assembled into larger bits until we get to the finished large unit, the text. Meaning is a problem in this approach. All theories have attempted to deal with meaning at the clause or sentence level. But the 'constituency view' breaks down decisively in the move from sentence to text.

The two views (text as formed in social practice vs. the constituency view of text) can be contrasted in a number of ways.

Here I will use two such contrasts. In the building-blocks model (the constituency view) there is an assumed prior intent (a kind of blueprint) which leads to the forming of the largest unit, the text. In the dynamic unfolding model (text as arising in social practice) there are social purposes which successively become realized, are changed, modulated, in line with the intentions of the makers. In the building-block model of text I might discover to my surprise after the event that someone else had made a text of a similar design. In the social, dynamic model I know: because language occurs as text, the 'materials' with which I am fashioning this interaction have been used before, I have encountered them in many social situations before, some similar, some different. The former theory needs some explanation to account for the occurence of similar or related texts, and for that it has invented the category of intertextuality (see Kristeva 1980, Bakhtin 1986, Moi (ed.) 1986, Fairclough 1992). The latter theory assumes from the beginning that I use materials which I have encountered before, which bear the meanings of their social contexts, to weave a new text which, because it is woven from materials of other texts, everywhere and always connects with those other texts.

This view raises the question of boundaries. In the weaving-notion of text (the metaphor connects with texture, textile) the flow and the dynamics of meaning in the complex social environments in which I find myself are the basis of text: a constantly shifting flow of meanings, in which meanings constantly alter in response to the dynamic of the wider social environment, constantly remade by those who participate in an interaction (imagine the ebb and flow, the dynamics of a lively conversation). This process of social meaning-making – of social semiosis – is what gives rise to the making of the text. But the boundaries of the text (set by social facts such as limits of time, significance of the issue, characteristics of the event, or of many other social purposes) are not the boundaries of meaning-making. I may go away and still ruminate, discuss in my head with myself, many of the things which were discussed in an interview, while the 'interview panel' is itself deliberating on that 'interview'. The text and its boundaries do not stop this process of semiosis: they provide a punctuation only – such as when the TV host of a debate says, 'Well, we haven't reached an agreement, but as we have run out of time, we'll leave that for now'. In this approach semiosis is ongoing, ceaseless: it is punctuated as textual forms, produced in the environments of particular social occasions.

This contrasts sharply with the building-block view, in which a pre-existing meaning is given formal expression in the manner in which I indicated earlier. If we see semiosis as ceaselessly ongoing (I can meet one of the participants of a conversation two weeks later and we can both immediately continue our debate), then both the relatedness and the connections of texts are unremarkable: they are what is normal, and no special term needs to be invented to name the situation. If we have a view of discrete complexes of meanings encoded in texts, and we find that other texts show similar features, then of course we need some theoretical category to account for this fact. 'Intertextuality' has become redundant as a theoretical term: its theoretical function now lies in the taken-for-granted assumption of the theory of semiosis; its specific functions are now carried by terms such as genre (and, in my own account, Foucauldian notions of discourse: Kress 1984/1989, Swales 1990, Fairclough 1992, Christie, Kress and Martin in Cope and Kalantzis (eds) 1993.

The view I am putting forward here has, however, some further ramifications. If the starting point is ceaseless semiosis which is given actualization/materialization in a particular social situation, then that has not actually settled the question of how the meanings should be actualized. That is, the common-sense view is that I express myself in or through language, because it is the medium of communication. But assume that I am using the medium of pen and paper, and the mode of graphic representation. I now have the choice of realizing some meanings through a diagram, others through writing. I have a choice of modes in which to 'fix' (using a metaphor from photography) my meanings. This shifts the theoretical ground from the assumption of expression through the one mode of language, to the assumption of expression through a multiplicity of modes.

This poses a severe challenge to common-sense notions of language, which have regarded it as the *full* medium of communication and as autonomous in respect to other modes (which are spoken of as *extra-* or *para*-linguistic). If, as in a live interaction, I have a multiplicity of modes available (the voice and its vast range of possibilities; my posture; gestures; facial expression; all of them used, by the way, as full means of articulation in the sign-languages of speech-impaired groups), my ability to use a variety of modes for 'fixing' meaning increases.

This immediately introduces a further question: could it be that one mode may be better than another for the communication of specific meanings? Could the spatial mode of images be better than the temporally based mode of speech for showing spatial relations between certain entities? Could the raised eyebrow be a better means of conveying irony than any word? In other words, we are moving here into the question of what semantic possibilities are 'afforded' by any one mode, and of course, with this we move to a direct challenge to any notion that language is a full medium of representation and communication.

There is another potential challenge here to notions of the 'integrity' of language: many of the features regarded as paralinguistic (voice-quality, use of pitch variation of certain kinds, rhythmic characteristics of the voice, etc.) are available for the 'fixing' of aspects of meaning. We need to ask therefore: do these form a part of what we think language is, or do they not? At the moment different linguistic theories give varying answers, though most will in fact exclude many or most of such features.

The issue of 'affordances', as much as that of what is in language and what is not, poses another, fundamental question: namely that of the relation between the material substance – the materiality – through which language is actualized and the kinds of meanings which are made. This can be raised at many different levels: is the sequential/temporal organization of speech-as-sound different in its semiotic potential from the spatial, hierarchical organization of writing-as-graphic substance? Is the potential of pitch-movement to form a question (by a rising intonation) the same as the potential for forming an interrogative by putting a question item in first position in a string of elements on the page ('*Who* killed Cock Robin?')?

What is at issue here is a decisive moving away from any idea of 'language as such', of meaning existing irrespective of its mode of actualization, where it had been entirely usual to speak of 'the same meaning' expressed in speech and in writing, or where we could assume that there is an easy translation between image and language.

In the following pages I will examine these issues in some detail. As I said at the beginning of the chapter, most of the points I am making here have been made before: it is the newer perspective of social semiotics which allows me to assemble them in this – at least potentially – productive fashion.

Pulling at some threads

As I have already suggested, and paradoxically perhaps, the category 'intertextuality' raises the most fundamental questions for the category 'text': in particular the two questions of the boundaries of text and of the constitution of the text – that is, the fundamental question 'What is a text?' Although in this chapter I will largely stay with these two concerns, one other obtrudes itself, namely the question of language itself. Intertextuality, it turns out, is a potently corrosive category for the hitherto seemingly settled question of what this thing 'language' may be. The metaphor of text may help to explain that problem, at least in part: intertextuality reinforces the metaphor of the 'weave' of text, and in doing so it raises the issue of what precisely are the threads of which this woven thing is made up. On the one hand, one part of the answer may turn out to be that these threads are much more than what we have come to think of as language alone; another part of the answer may be that language itself turns out to be an entirely insecurely established phenomenon.

Let me begin by looking at a quite simple text. It is now, at the time that I write this chapter, some seven years old. It comes from a particular social occasion, a by-election for a seat on the local government in a town in the north of England. The political party to which this candidate belonged no longer exists in this form. In other words, the text was produced – like every text – in a particular moment, in a particular place, under particular circumstances. It is an object produced as the result of a complex set of interlocking social actions; and in that respect too it is like all texts. Some elements of that interlocking set of social actions can be recovered from the text itself. They are there as traces. I will mention a few only, simply as a means of indicating the kind of thing I have in mind. There is an issue of national politics, the 'poll tax' so-called; this was an issue which aroused the most widespread debate and action: it constituted an element of significance in the life of all adult members of British society at the time. There is the event of the local election, which gives rise most immediately to the production of this text. There are the various events referred to in the text, some relatively permanent – the fact that there are car parks, for instance, and people employed to count the money collected in these car parks; there are salary rises and 'squeezed' household budgets, etc.

FOCUS

AXE THE POLL TAX

Household budgets continue to be squeezed by the excessive demands of the Poll Tax. Janie Kirkman shares the widespread feeling of anger against this unjust tax and wants to see it replaced by a Local Income Tax, which would be fairer and cheaper:

FAIRER because it is related to ability to pay,
CHEAPER because it costs less to collect.

But until it is scrapped, what can be done to bring the Poll Tax down?

Lancaster City Council must play its part by cutting out waste and promoting greater efficiency, but it is responsible for only 10% of the bill, and so cannot have much impact on the total.

But the government could help by restoring the 1.16 million it chopped from this year's grant.

The County Council could contribute by holding down the massive salary rises it gives to its chief officers and the generous perks that go to county councillors (meals subsidised by over 1,200,000 last year).

In Lancaster, we need to look at all job vacancies, try to slim down the administration and take advantage of new technology. Do we really need to employ 37 people to count the cash from the city's carparks? Could this not be automated? Janie Kirkman believes that greater efficiency could produce savings and keep the Poll Tax down.

CONSULTING PEOPLE FIRST

4 Poll tax flyer

The point is that there is, in the community which is constituted at least temporarily by the recipients of this text, an ongoing flow of issues, there is ongoing *semiosis*.

Elements of this semiosis are represented in this text via a set of specifically textual practices. There is, for instance, the practice of 'reporting' and its various attendant transformations. The textual elements assembled in this text all existed at some earlier stage in this process of semiosis, as elements of other texts; they are here in variously transformed manner. For instance, the sentence 'Janie Kirkman shares the widespread feeling of anger ...' reports a prior utterance, in another text, in which J.K. perhaps said something like, 'I share the anger everyone feels; I think this tax is totally unjust'. While this 'intertextual connection' is quite clear here in relation to this element of indirect reported speech, it is also present in more heavily transformed elements. For instance, in the paragraph which begins 'Lancaster City Council ...' there is the textual remnant – to look at it from one point of view – of a dialogic text: Councillor X: 'We in Lancaster City Council will have to play our part in cutting out waste. We can and must promote yet greater efficiencies.' Councillor Y: 'However much we cut, we are only responsible for 10 per cent of the total expenditure, so our savings can have only limited impact', etc. Clearly in this case the transformation of prior textual elements is heavier, largely because it is likely to be the result of a *series* of intervening transformations via other texts; whereas J.K.'s speech (whether invented/fictional or actual/factual) has been subject to the transformative action of one textual agent only, namely that of the reporter/writer of this text.

On the one hand there is a set of interlocking social actions (themselves embedded in webs of social structures of various kinds, extent and size), and these constitute the stuff of an ongoing process of social semiosis. On the other hand this semiosis is constantly textualized – that is, it is realized in the material form of language, as texts of various kinds. This textualization/realization is always transformative in various ways. Generically, for instance, J.K.'s direct speech – which may have been part of an *interview* – becomes indirect reported speech, part of a *feature article* of a peculiar sort in an election pamphlet masquerading as a local newspaper. A *debate* in the context of a council meeting – let us assume – appears in a more heavily transformed fashion as part of this feature article/report. On the one hand social semiosis is textually open, in as much as it can be textualized in quite distinctly differing ways; on the other hand it is always textually specific, in that its conditions of emergence are always tied to particular textual generic form, in specific semiotic modes.

Several points emerge here. The notion of intertextuality which implicitly underpins my analysis is a radical one, in the sense that it treats *all texts as always constituted of transformed elements of other, prior texts*. This is a notion of text which takes text-as-'weave' radically seriously: (all) text is always constituted out of elements of other texts, which in the process of constituting the new text are transformed in line with the generic requirements of the new text. This is a fundamental challenge to notions of the generation/production of text which might have emerged out of structuralist accounts of language: versions of constituency views of language, that is, views of text as generated newly out of the syntactic categories and rules of a language. To state this explicitly: text is not formed from sequences of sentences generated out of the syntactic capacities of a grammatical system; rather, text is made of elements – more or less transformed – of other texts. This poses a radical challenge to notions of 'the language system', whether in structuralist or in functionalist theories of language. This is where the concept of intertextuality, produced to solve problems in an a-textual theory of language, poses its fundamental challenge to mainstream theories of language, and where it points to the need for a radically new, *text-based social theory of language,* and for a new conception of semiosis.

There is, at the same time, a conservative notion of intertextuality at work in this analysis: the transformative work performed on the elements of other texts in the constitution of the new text works in one direction, namely in the direction of the assumed generic forms of (other) existing texts – in this case in the direction of the genre of feature article/report. So while the elements of the text come from diverse textual sources, and undergo transformation of a more or less extensive kind, the shape of the newly produced text draws on or leans on the understood shape of other, existing texts. Intertextually, most readers will recognize the generic/textual similarity of this text to others which they have encountered before – that after all is what will make this text 'work'. With some prodding, most readers will also recognize the textual origins or antecedents of elements of the text. In other words, in its internal constitution this text draws from semiotic resources in all their diverse textualization. In its overall shape this text leans – 'intergenerically' – on the understood shape of texts of a similar kind. In its constitution it operates both transgenerically (and works to obliterate the traces of its prior textual origins) and intragenerically (and works to affirm the stability of textual types).

If one sense of intertextuality is that of 'reference to other texts', then another use is that of 'transformation of prior text'. In most instances, given the conventions of text-production in many (though by no means *all*) domains of 'Western' society (that is,

demands for 'novelty', 'creativity', etc.) this transforï
works to obliterate traces of the prior textual form of tl
the new text. In many domains successful production
on precisely this ability: in academic writing, for instanᵤₑ,
taining the difficult line between 'plagiarism' and 'saying it in your
own words'.

The radical approach to intertextuality places semiosis as prior
to its textual instantiation; the conservative approach to intertextuality places textual form prior to semiosis, as a confining frame for
semiosis. In each case text acts as a punctuation of semiosis. The
process of semiosis is momentarily brought to standstill in textual
form.

Textual forms: the boundaries of text

The issue of the boundaries of a text are raised sharply both by the
concept of intertextuality and by a definition of text as the punctuation of semiosis. The 'radical notion' in any case sees semiosis as
working with previously textualized materials in producing new
texts; the conservative notion sees continuities between one text
and another and between kinds of text. My discussion so far has
implicitly proceeded from the point of view of production, where
the maker of the text sets the boundaries of the text. However, those
are not necessarily the boundaries set or accepted by the reader of
the text.

To take again the text I have been discussing so far. What are
the boundaries of this text? One answer is to say that the text
consists of the headline 'Axe The Poll Tax' and all of the verbal text
below it – though probably without the conspicuous words
'Consulting People First'. This sets one kind of boundary, produced
by a sense of completeness, however established.

Within this text are some generically differing elements, for
instance the two slogans 'Fairer ...', 'Cheaper ...'. The shifts in the
mode of addressing the reader, from the report-like opening paragraph to the exhortatory last paragraph, also point to variation
generically speaking. A genre – though not a text – is characterized,
among other things, by a stability of mode of address – or, better, by
a stability of the social relations of the participants in a linguistic
interaction. This points to an important factor: the boundaries of the
text are not necessarily the boundaries of a genre. Within this rela-

ιvely brief text there are several shifts in the implied or expressed social relations of the 'participants' – that is, of writer and reader: the report-relation of paragraph 1; the slogan-address; the rhetorical question of paragraph 3; the 'suggestions' of paragraphs 4 and 5; the exhortation of paragraph 6.

Each shift marks one kind of generic segment and is one kind of intratextual punctuation. It is therefore one kind of boundary, marking off one set of social relations, one kind of social occasion from another. But the text overall has two other kinds of boundaries, one abstract/textual and one material/textual. The abstract/textual boundary is marked by the 'masthead', which declares that this text is to be read as the mock front page of a mock local newspaper: it, together with a verbal–visual logo 'Social and Liberal Democrats', which appears in the original pamphlet, is essential to a full reading of this text. Without these a reader would have little 'anchorage' for her or his reading; together they announce that this is an election pamphlet and declare the political party to which the candidate who is seeking election belongs.

While the producer of the text may not regard this as an essential part of the text, or part of the text at all, for the reader this is crucial information, and in a sense so important as to make the rest of the text nearly redundant. For the reader therefore the boundaries of the text are likely to be different than they are for the producer. This is a crucial matter, which bears on the issue of intertextuality in at least two ways. In terms of the readers' location in their social world, it establishes connections with a domain of semiosis (and of its textualization) which provides essential means for reading. Simply, if I know that I am reading a party-political text my reading is influenced by that; if I know which party has produced the material my reading is, again, influenced and shaped. Both provide me with information which allows me to connect this text with others, and equally allows me to set it off from many others. Being located in a particular domain of semiosis, and of text, is essential for full readings. This is a general rule and holds as much here as it holds for newspapers in general, or for any text at all. The second factor also has to do with where the boundary is placed, for that determines whether my reading is of one text with internal complexities, or of two texts which I have to bring into conjunction.

The second boundary is the straightforwardly material one. The *page* provides a clear frame; it is a bounded entity, a visual–material unit. Moreover, the page is just so big and no bigger. That seems too banal a point to be worth making: yet both of these factors have significant consequences. The fact that the page is a clearly demarcated *visual* unit means that elements within this unit are likely to be treated as being a part of that unit, as being semiotically connected and therefore to be read together. This is likely to be the case both from the producer's and from the reader's point of view. It makes it possible, for instance, to read the masthead and the logo as part of the one text. While this may not seem highly significant – or decisive – here, for many newspaper, magazine or textbook pages this becomes a crucial matter. The various, seemingly clearly bounded, texts on the page of a newspaper or magazine can be read together, deliberately or not, to produce textual units of larger or different kinds than those marked off in other ways. So for instance many contemporary magazine pages use this visual means of layout to blur a textual-generic distinction which was rigidly maintained as recently as, say, twenty years ago, namely that between feature article and advertising. This has led to new generic forms which seemed entirely illegitimate socially and textually two decades ago – blurring the social positions of reader and of consumer, of fact and fiction, of information and advertising, etc. In other words the maintenance of textual boundaries has social origins and social consequences; and so does the blurring of these boundaries. Here intertextuality can be seen as a category with strong ideological, social and political effects.

The existence of specific kinds of (extra- and intra-) textual punctuation has social origins and social motivations; and it is the existence of such punctuations which makes possible new, yet again socially motivated fusions and other new formations. This shows again the central role of text in any understanding of the processes of language and of social actions alike.

The second material boundary is that of size. If the page as a unit provides one kind of framing within which elements can be and are read together (including elements which are meant by their producers to function as integrally distinct *texts*), then size provides another framing of equal though different importance. To take the 'Focus' text as an example once more. It is formed by folding an A4-size sheet in half. This produces several textually and generically important effects. Instead of the single A4 *sheet* (with a back and a front) there are now four *pages*: a front page, a back page and two inside pages. This material action immediately changes the generic potential of this piece of paper: from its potential, as *newsletter*, perhaps, to a potential as *newspaper* (with front page, pages 2 and 3, etc.). A *front page* is an already existing generic/textual form and opens up the possibility of types of text appropriate to a front page (and similarly of course for the other pages). In other words, one consequence of the material fact of size is generic – not only here of course, but generally speaking. A one-hour slot for speaking is generically different from a five-minute slot: on radio, for instance, the latter can be the 'Thought for the day'; the former can be the lecture by the distinguished public figure.

In terms of punctuation of semiosis, the size of the frame has precisely this effect, generically; but it also has the effect of producing different kinds of selection of material from the flow of semiosis. The social–cultural valuation, furthermore, of the text of the five-minute slot is different from that of the sixty-minute one.

To give another instance of this intricate connection of materiality, genericness and textuality, consider two examples of 'newspapers' produced by two children: one at the age of 4 years 9 months (figure 5), the other at the age of 7 years (figure 6).

5 Child (4 years, 9 months) draws newspaper

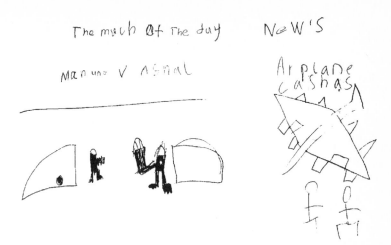

6 Child (7 years) draws newspaper

Both are readings of what a newspaper is (and both need to be seen in the context of a developmental 'chain' which begins much earlier as quite another reading, and continues for a considerable time). The first was produced using an A4 sheet; it clearly has a notion of 'a page', and of the structure of a page: it has a verbal text (here indicated as bold headlines) and an image below it. The second example is produced using a *folded* A4 sheet, as in the 'Focus' example: an innovation produced by this young text-maker for himself. Here too this material act has much the same generic consequences: it produces a front page, two inside pages and a back page. It is quite clear that this material act fosters for the child a sense of genre: there is a sports page and a news page, and on both there are the quite clear beginnings of generically apt language.

Of course, the division of sports page and news page reflects another socially produced organization of semiosis, namely that of 'contents' and the social forming of content – using Foucauldian terminology, organization of content as *discourse* (Foucault 1971). I regard this not as a punctuation – it does not produce textual *units* – but as an organization of the semiotic material which has its emergence in textual form. Of course, just as there is intertextuality (and 'intergenericness') so there will be 'interdiscursivity' – reference in one text to discursive materials from other texts. In the 'Focus' text, for instance, phrases like 'massive salary rises', 'generous perks', 'excessive demands' are not only intertextual in their reference to other texts in which these terms will have occurred but are discursively specific: they have their place here and refer implicitly and indirectly to other discourses, in which the salary rises are no doubt referred to differently, perhaps as 'necessary rewards for effort'.

Materiality of text: semiosis in visual and verbal form

In considering the page (as well as the *text*) as one of the significant punctuations of semiosis we have turned from abstract categories to material ones, and, at the same time, from a concern with language alone to a concern with other modes of representation, in this case the visual (as well as the material of paper itself). Implicit in (most) debates on intertextuality is an assumption about text as being verbally realized, or of semiosis as dependent on the mode of language. Semiosis occurs in a multiplicity of modes, even though this is not (fully) acknowledged in 'official' theories of text. Language is one realizational means of semiosis among many. If text is a *punctuation* of semiosis (or one of various punctuational means), then the various semiotic modes are different means of *fixing* semiosis. In a period when texts are in any case becoming increasingly and more insistently multimodal – that is, realized in several semiotic modes – it is becoming essential to pay attention not only to the forms of semiosis (its punctuations) but also to its realizational means (its 'fixing').

This provides two distinct ways of thinking about semiosis and text: in terms of realization(al) means and in terms of punctuations. The latter gives rise to the various kinds of linguistic and textual segmental categories which are well known: genres, paragraphs, sentences and 'below-sentence' categories such as phrases of various kinds; the former gives rise to realizational modes of various forms, which have hardly received attention, certainly not in linguistic approaches to text. With the increasing prominence of multimodal textual forms, and in particular of textual forms which have as their realizational mode both the visual and the verbal, it becomes imperative to pay serious attention to these new kinds of textual form. If the text/punctuations have social causes and effects, the different realizational modes offer – or so it seems at this stage – distinctly different potentials of representation, and consequently quite distinctive cognitive and affective possibilities. In other words, it may well be the case that the material characteristics of a semiotic mode have certain 'affordances' and certain limitations, so that not everything can be represented in any mode, or at least not with equal facility. The sequential/temporal characteristic of language-as-speech may lend itself with greater facility to the representation of action and sequences of action; while the spatial display of visual images may lend itself with greater facility to the representation of elements and their relation to each other.

In figure 7 it may be that some specialization of the visual and the verbal modes in relation to the processes of semiosis is already apparent. The page is from a science textbook for the middle years of secondary school. The language is simple; most sentences are one-clause sentences, a few are two-clause sentences. They are to do with actions and events: actions and events that have happened, or which the textbook instructs the students to undertake.

The contrast with a pre-war textbook (figure 8) is startling. Consider the final paragraph for comparison.

> The simple electric motor consists of a coil pivoted between the poles of a permanent magnet (see Fig. 63). When a current is passed through the coil in the direction indicated in the figure we can show, by applying Fleming's left-hand rule, that the left-hand side of the coil will tend to move down and the right-hand side to move up. (Remember that the direction of the field due to the permanent magnet is from the N. to the S. pole.) Thus the coil will rotate in a counter-clockwise direction to a vertical position.

This language is much more complex syntactically. The second sentence in this paragraph contains about seven clauses (depending on the type of grammar adopted in parsing), integrated in the sentence through the syntactic means of subordination/embedding of various kinds. That is one clear difference between the two texts. Another, more significant, is that in the earlier text all the curricular information which the students are meant to know is carried by the language. There is an illustration on the page on which this sentence occurs: but it is just that – an illustration. That is, it shows, it repeats in visual form (or at least that is the intention) the information provided by the language. The illustration is not meant to add information, merely to reinforce it. In the contemporary textbook, the situation is entirely different. Here the images do not function as illustrations: they do not simply repeat in visual form

12·9 *Electronics*

Circuits

In your first circuits you used torch bulbs joined with wires. Modern electrical equipment uses the same basic ideas. But if you look inside a computer there are not many wires or torch bulbs. The wires and bulbs have been replaced by electronic devices like transistors, chips and light-emitting diodes.

Transistors and chips are examples of *semiconductors*. They are made from special crystals like silicon. Transistors work because they only conduct electricity in the right conditions. They are useful because they can turn on and off very fast, and they need very little electricity.

An electronic light

● You can make electronic circuits with wires like the circuits you made before. The difficulty is that the contacts are poor, and sometimes things do not work. It is far better to *solder* the components.

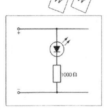

Here is a simple circuit to operate a light-emitting diode (LED).

This design shows the same circuit soldered on matrix board. The board is cheap and can be reused.

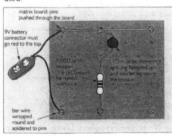

Transistors

A transistor is a special semi-conductor. It has three connections: a base, a collector and an emitter. When a small current is put on the base, it lets a much larger current flow between the collector and the emitter. So a tiny current can control a much larger one.

● Try this water-detector circuit.

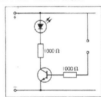

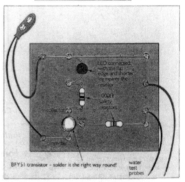

When the probes touch something wet, a very small current goes from the battery through the water to the base of the transistor. This current is big enough to make the transistor work, so the LED lights up.

140

7 Science textbook 1988: electronics

76   MAGNETISM AND ELECTRICITY

the magnetic poles. Fig. 62(c) shows the combined field of (a) and (b) when the wire is placed between the poles.

Note that, in Fig. 62(a) and (b), the lines of force on the left of the wire are in the same direction as those of the external field, while those on the right of the wire are in the opposite direction. Consequently in the combined field of Fig. 62(c) the field to the left of the wire is strong—there are a large number of lines, while the field to the right is weak.

If we assume, with Faraday, that the lines of force are in tension and trying to shorten (see p. 18), we should expect the wire to be urged to the right. This is precisely what we find by experiment.

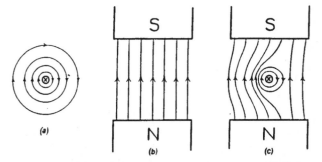

Fig. 62. (a) Magnetic field due to current in straight wire. (b) Field due to magnetic poles. (c) Combined field of (a) and (b).

The principle of the electric motor.

The simple electric motor consists of a coil pivoted between the poles of a permanent magnet (see Fig. 63). When a current is passed through the coil in the direction indicated in the figure we can show, by applying Fleming's left-hand rule, that the left-hand side of the coil will tend to move down and the right-hand side to move up. (Remember that the direction of the field due to the permanent magnet is from the N. to the S. pole.) Thus the coil will rotate in a counter-clockwise direction to a vertical position.

8 Science textbook 1936: magnetism and electricity

information already provided by the language. The images provide *new* and *different* information. Whereas the written language is concerned with actions and events, the image is concerned to show the structure, and the internal structural relations, of, in this case, a circuit, of *the content at issue*. Language does one job: it recounts, narrates, and instructs; the image does another: it displays the content and its internal structure.

As far as the question of intertextuality is concerned, we need to adopt one of two positions: we can either say that in figure 8 we have two texts, which stand in a close relation to each other, between which there are strong 'phoric' relations; or we can say that we have one text, in which semiotic processes are realized verbally and visually. Each of these positions poses its problems and points in certain directions. Taking the 'two-texts' route leads us in a direction in which we need to develop a theory in which semiosis realized in the verbal mode can be related to semiosis realized in the visual mode. This entails developing means of description in which semiotic objects ('texts') in two modes can be dealt with and brought into conjunction descriptively and theoretically. Given that this route assumes that the verbal text is not complete by itself – that is, that no adequate reading can be given of it in isolation – it becomes a task for a theory of verbal text, and therefore for a theory of language, to concern itself with the development of such a theory and its descriptive/analytical forms.

In other words, the concept of intertextuality cannot remain a language-dependent concept alone if we adopt the two-text route. If however we adopt the 'one-text' route, then the consequences become more severe for a theory of verbal text and for a theory of language. In fact, that route will force us to abandon a theory of text as a verbal object; indeed it will force us to abandon the possibility of a theory of verbal text, and it will explode the notion of 'language' as an integral phenomenon. The reasons are straightforward: if, as a normal procedure of accounting for 'text', I have to consider issues which have so far been included in theories of (linguistic) text as well as issues which have so far formed no part at all of such a theory, then I no longer have an integral notion either of text as a verbal object or of language as a representationally or communica-tionally integral phenomenon.

In the case of figure 8 it seems clear to me that we need to take the 'one-text' route, with all its consequences. The verbal and visual elements are so tightly integrated that no other possibility offers itself. This forces us into considering the existence of a new 'code' which consists of visual and verbal elements which are used according to 'rules of aptness' – in this case verbal realization for events or actions, and visual realization for elements and their (spatial) relations (whether metaphorically spatial or 'actually' spatial). However, once this is recognized it has knock-on effects for other instances; again, I think of the pages of newspapers or magazines (or television screens where a voice-over goes with a visually presented account; and this of course has been the case for a considerable time now with the medium of film), where 'texts' whether verbal or visual co-exist side-by-side. There are of course conventions for reading (and conventions for production) more or less stringently enforced, which attempt to regulate how we are to make sense of such pages. However, the present period is one where practices of text-production are changing at a faster pace than practices of the production of rules for reading, so that the older rules no longer work.

Multimodal landscape of communication and the concept of intertextuality

I suggested above that the producer of the 'Focus' text may not have intended the masthead and the logo (two over-lapping squares, with the name of the party printed over the front square) to be part of the 'text' of this front page. Of course, if this is so it leaves the question of the purpose of this residue-text (masthead plus logo) for the maker of the text. The logo itself suggests, through the overlapping squares, the 'coming together' of two separate entities. Placing the logo at the top right corner of the page may therefore have a function designed more for the members of a newly formed party than for other readers; and similarly with the masthead. This would legitimate treating the front page as consisting of two texts. The fact that one of these 'texts' is a visual much more than a verbal object, or that its major content – the recent merging of two formerly separate political parties – is visually expressed, fits with my assertion about the visual realization of semiosis as one entirely usual mode. The page, whether considered as one text or as two (or indeed as three, if we regard the band at the bottom as yet another distinct text-element), can only be read fully if it is regarded as a multimodal semiotic entity. As I suggested before, in either case there are severe problems for a conventional theory of text; and in this last section I will review them briefly.

The concept of intertextuality takes as its starting point the existence of formal categories of language – text, for instance – and proposes to deal with the problem of the connectedness of texts from that position. This approach produces a new set of problems not only for a theory of text but for a form-based theory of language. In particular, two problems arise, namely that of the boundaries of texts and that of relations between semiotic modes. An alternative position is to start from the processes of semiosis and to ask two fundamental questions: in what mode do semiotic processes get realized ('fixed'); and what are the punctuations of the process of semiosis? The former question points to conventions of cultural uses of semiotic modes, and to existing specializations, as well as to historically changing uses and specializations. It assumes that semiosis is by no means restricted to the mode of language. In fact it challenges accepted notions of language as a stable, homogeneous entity, and treats the phenomenon of language as itself an amalgam of a multiplicity of semiotic modes. The question of what semiotic modes are in use also points to the issue of the capacities and limitations of modes, and the cognitive and affective affordances and limitations of each.

The second question, about the punctuations of semiosis, is a question about individuals, their cognitive and affective work, set in the context of social practices and their structures and regularities: that approach takes semiosis itself as relatively unbounded, as both individual and social, and in large degree free to take whatever modal realization is apt and to take its overt structurings, boundaries and punctuations from the contingencies of social practices and the conventions which surround them. These punctuations are guided by existing forms (genres, for instance) but not fully so: there is a tension between the processes of semiosis and the social occasions which provide the framing of semiosis. These punctuations also provide new objects – texts – which are momentary congealings of semiosis, and as such provide new elements and new resources for the further processes of ongoing semiosis. Although I have not referred to this in my discussion here, these punctuations of semiosis, and the framings produced, operate both at the level of text and at levels below the text: the sentence is, in this view, an element produced as a result of the text-level punctuations of semiosis.

Arising from the issue of 'punctuations of semiosis' is that of the *kinds* of punctuations which are produced, facilitated, valued, made possible or ruled out. In so far as the framing shapes what is in the frame, as a new conceptual/social/cultural/semiotic entity, it is important *what* kinds of entities are available, what their conceptual/semiotic contents are, what they make possible and what they inhibit or rule out. The two issues of *semiotic mode of realization* and *kinds of punctuation* together set parameters to the semiotic resources available to individuals in a culture and to that culture. They also set parameters, invisibly but tellingly, to the processes of synaesthesia – the cognitive/neural 'trade' and work which goes on incessantly in the silent making of 'internally' formed signs.

Conclusion

Intertextuality is a concept which arises in a language-based understanding of text, within a theory of language focused on linguistic form – a clause-and-sentence-based grammar struggling to deal with the category of text. By proposing the connectedness of texts it puts the category of text itself into crisis; by pointing to the semantic connectedness of texts it focuses on the processes of semiosis and points away from the form-based starting point of most linguistic theories. By making text prior – text as produced out of elements of prior texts – it puts into crisis the structuralist/generativist notions of the generation of linguistic form.

The category of intertextuality is produced to solve a problem for form-based constituency theories of language and language-based notions of text. Its effects are to focus on the processes of semiosis as prior, and to lead to a new view not just of text but of language. Semiosis is not restricted to a material realization in language alone; nor is text a purely or solely linguistic entity. From a starting point of attempting to solve the problems of a form-based theory of language and of a language-based notion of text the implications of the concept move us to a position that treats social semiosis as prior, sees text as always multimodal, treats text as the focal formal unit of social-semiotic punctuation, and treats certain below-textual formal units (paragraphs, sentences, clauses, phrases – that is, syntactically formal units, though this even includes morpho-lexemic units) as formed in that process of textual punctuation. It pushes us to a notion of communication in which social semiosis is prior and is always multimodal, and in which text is the focal unit and is generative of all other units.

But then in the new semiotic landscapes which most post-industrial societies are entering, an age in which the new forms of economics will be centred on 'information' as both raw material and commodity, in which the globalized media are based on new electronically supported modes of text-production – multimedia for instance, based on the resources of 'hypertext' – that new theory of semiosis is overdue.

References and Bibliography

Bakhtin. M. (1986), *Speech Genres and Other Essays*, Austin: University of Texas Press.

Cope, B. and Kalantzis, M. (eds) (1993), *The Powers of Literacy*, London: Falmer Press.

Fairclough, N. (1992), *Discourse and Social Change*, Oxford: Polity Press.

Foucault, M. (1971), 'Orders of discourse', *Social Science Information* 10.2: 7–30.

Foucault, M. (1972), *The Archeology of Knowledge* (trans. M. Sheridan Smith), London: Tavistock.

Halliday, M. A. K. (1978), *Language as a Social Semiotic*, London: Edward Arnold.

Halliday, M. A. K. (1985), *An Introduction to Functional Grammar*, London: Edward Arnold.

Hodge, R. I. V. and Kress, G. R. (1988), *Social Semiotics*, Oxford: Polity Press.

Kress, G. R. (1984/1989), *Linguistic Processes in Sociocultural Practices*, Geelong/Oxford: Deakin University Press/Oxford University Press.

Kress, G. R. (1993), 'Against arbitrariness: the social production of the sign as a foundational issue in critical discourse analysis', *Discourse and Society* 4.2: 169–93.

Kress, G. R. (1997), *Before Writing: Rethinking the Paths to Literacy*, London: Routledge.

Kristeva, J. (1980), *Desire in Language* (trans. T. Gora, A. Jardine, L. Roudiez), New York: Columbia University Press.

Moi, T. (ed.) (1986), *The Kristeva Reader*, Oxford: Basil Blackwell.

Swales, J. (1990), *Genre Analysis*, Cambridge: Cambridge University Press.

Voloshinov, V. N. (1973), *Marxism and the Philosophy of Language*, New York: Seminar Press.

Index